PERGAMON INSTITUTE OF ENGLISH (OXFORD)

English Language Teaching Documents

General Editor: C. J. Brumfit

LANGUAGE TEACHING PROJECTS
FOR
THE THIRD WORLD

The British Council ELT Documents — Back Issues

LANGUAGE TEACHING PROJECTS
FOR
THE THIRD WORLD

Edited by

C. J. BRUMFIT
University of London Institute of Education

ELT Documents 116

Published in association with
THE BRITISH COUNCIL
by
PERGAMON PRESS
Oxford · New York · Toronto · Sydney · Paris · Frankfurt

U.K.	Pergamon Press Ltd., Headington Hill Hall, Oxford OX3 0BW, England
U.S.A.	Pergamon Press Inc., Maxwell House, Fairview Park, Elmsford, New York 10523, U.S.A.
CANADA	Pergamon Press Canada Ltd., Suite 104, 150 Consumers Road, Willowdale, Ontario M2J 1P9, Canada
AUSTRALIA	Pergamon Press (Aust.) Pty. Ltd., P.O. Box 544, Potts Point, N.S.W. 2011, Australia
FRANCE	Pergamon Press SARL, 24 rue des Ecoles, 75240 Paris, Cedex 05, France
FEDERAL REPUBLIC OF GERMANY	Pergamon Press GmbH, Hammerweg 6, D-6242 Kronberg-Taunus, Federal Republic of Germany

First edition 1983

Library of Congress Cataloging in Publication Data

Main entry under title:
Language teaching projects for the Third World.
(ELT documents; 116)
1. English language—Study and teaching—Foreign speakers.
2. English language—Study and teaching—Underdeveloped areas. 3. Underdeveloped areas—Education.
I. Brumfit, Christopher. II. Series: English language teaching documents; 116.
PE1128.A2L3 1983   428′ .007′ 01724   83-8172

British Library Cataloguing in Publication Data

Language teaching projects for the Third World.
(English language teaching documents; 116)
1. English language—Study and teaching—
Underdeveloped areas   2. Curriculum planning
I. Brumfit, C. J.   II. Series
428.2′ 4′ 071   PE1128
ISBN 0-08-030342-0

Printed in Great Britain by
Redwood Burn Ltd   Trowbridge, Wiltshire

EDITOR'S PREFACE

WESTERN governments are increasingly committed to giving aid in the form of specific projects with clearly identified goals and limited objectives. Clearly, there are many advantages in this system, for both parties to the aid agreement then know exactly what is expected in provision of time, finance, personnel and so on. Yet in many spheres, including education, our mutual needs may not be clearly identifiable, our objectives may be too long-term to fit neatly into the project model, and the concentration of expertise into those areas that donor countries possess greatest strength it may distort the needs of the recipients. If we are successfully to evaluate the experience of working with projects, whether to improve subsequent projects or to question or modify the whole concept, we need clear reports of the problems, difficulties and successes in existing activity. This collection of papers, concentrating on project work in Africa, but with general implications for all North–South relations, is designed to contribute to such clarification. Most of the projects reported originate with British Council support, and nearly all the contributions relate their own specific requirements to the state of theory in needs analysis, implementation and evaluation. Sometimes basic questions of the role that English can and should play in the life of particular countries need to be confronted. All of these papers address themselves, in various ways, to the interface between theory and practice.

The order of papers is approximately in ascending level of sophistication of English required, from primary to advanced professional.

C J BRUMFIT

CONTENTS

THE ROLE AND STATUS OF ENGLISH AS A SUBJECT IN THE ZAMBIAN ENGLISH-MEDIUM CONTEXT

ROY WIGZELL

Department of Literature and Languages, University of Zambia

Introduction

In nearly all the former British colonies in Africa, English continues to be used as a medium of instruction at some stage in the school system. Since it is nowhere widely used by the indigenous population as the language of the home, its use as a medium is crucially dependent upon its being taught effectively as a subject in the schools. In no case, however, can it be confidently asserted that English as a subject has succeeded in adequately meeting the demands of English as a medium. The available evidence suggests that all the Anglophone countries of black Africa have experienced severe educational problems directly attributable to the use of an alien language as the medium of instruction. Most of the countries concerned have tried to alleviate the problems by delaying the introduction of English as a medium until the upper grades of the primary school or the lower grades of the secondary school and by providing basic primary education in a local indigenous language. Only three countries – the Gambia, Sierra Leone and Zambia – have remained firmly committed to a universal English-medium policy. The present paper focuses on the situation in Zambia, where, after an intensive public debate on the medium issue, English has been given a renewed mandate to serve as the sole medium of instruction for most subjects throughout the educational system (cf. Zambia Ministry of Education, 1977).

My purpose in reviewing the ELT situation in Zambia is not to reopen the medium issue but rather to direct attention once again towards the role and status of English as a subject and its effectiveness in meeting the demands of English as a medium. In the first part of the paper I shall present a description and evaluation of the English language programmes currently offered at the three educational levels. My main concern at this stage will be to account for the gap that appears to have opened up between the standard of proficiency that the teaching of English as a subject is able to achieve under the present regime and that which the use of English as a medium presupposes. In the ensuing section I shall report briefly on projects that are planned or already under way for the revision or development of existing courses and then proceed to consider a number of alternative strategies that might more effectively narrow the gap between English as a subject and

1

English as a medium. Finally, and by way of conclusion, however, I shall want to suggest that if the English-medium policy is to succeed in achieving its primary objective of facilitating learning,[1] the mutual dependency and complementarity of English as a subject and English as a medium needs to be recognized and more systematically exploited than it has been hitherto.

1.   The existing ELT programme

As a result of a Cabinet decision taken in 1965 in favour of English-medium,[2] an English Medium Centre under the direction of a British Aid to Commonwealth English officer was set up with the task of producing an English-medium primary course. The original intention was to adapt the *New Peak Course*, which had been developed specifically for use in Kenya. Just as the process of adaptation got under way, however, the results of an evaluation of the *New Peak Course* were released, from which the Centre concluded that the course (though not the policy underlying it) was a failure. It was therefore dropped as a basis for the Zambian course and work was begun on a completely new course, which took the best part of seven years to complete but which was hurriedly introduced into the schools in stages as each set of units was completed. The first units, indeed, were already being introduced into Lusaka schools as early as 1966. The English Medium Centre itself recommended a gradual phasing in of what was intended to be only an experimental version of the course, arguing that the failure of the *New Peak Course* was due primarily to the fact that it had been introduced into the system too rapidly (cf. Higgs, *op. cit.*). Ministry Headquarters, however, anxious for political reasons to show early development on a broad front in education, pressed for the rapid expansion of English medium throughout the system. By 1975 about 75 per cent of primary schools were using what was still considered to be an experimental version of a course that had never been modified in the light of evaluation. The same experimental version is now in use in virtually every class of every school in the country.

As it now stands, the primary English course contains an English language reading component, each consisting of teachers' handbooks supported by course readers and, at the more advanced levels, by supplementary readers. One or two pupils' workbooks were produced early on but these are no longer in use. The teachers' handbooks, which constitute in effect the syllabus, are highly prescriptive and set out in detail the content and methodology of each teaching unit throughout the entire seven-year course. This strictly controlled approach was arguably necessary at a time when the majority of primary school teachers were untrained Form 3 drop-outs, but it is becoming increasingly inappropriate as the proportion of untrained teachers still in the system gets progressively smaller. As it was originally designed, the course did not explicitly identify any objectives. Conscious of a deficiency in this respect, the Curriculum Development Centre (the successor of the English Medium Centre) published in 1978 a detailed set of objectives extrapolated from the handbooks but specified in structural rather than behavioural terms to match the content of the handbooks. There is still no explicit indication anywhere in the course material, therefore, of what the pupils are expected to be able to do with the language at the end of the programme.

The primary English course as a whole places much greater emphasis upon the development of reading skills than upon the development of writing skills. The course, indeed, is seriously deficient in all types of writing exercises (cf. Chishimba, 1979). Reading comprehension work, moreover, is based almost entirely on multiple-choice exercises reflecting the format of the final Grade 7 examination. Being computer marked, the final examination offers little or no scope for the assessment of creative writing skills, and this deficiency in the examination is inevitably reflected in the teaching in the upper primary grades. The overall result is that by the end of the course, the ability of the pupils to express themselves correctly and creatively in writing is seriously underdeveloped. By comparison, the reading skills of the majority of the pupils seem to be relatively well developed.[3] There are grounds for believing, however, that as a direct result of English medium a significant minority of pupils fail to learn to read at all.

Although the primary English course was considered from the outset to be experimental, it did not have any built-in evaluation procedure. A small-scale evaluation of the course was conducted in Lusaka schools in 1967 but the results were ignored because it was felt that there were no criteria to relate the results to (cf. Higgs, *op. cit.*). Following reports that some Grade 7 leavers were illiterate, the Psychological Services Department of the Ministry of Education conducted a survey in 1973 of the reading skills of over 3000 Grade 3 pupils. The report concluded that 'the course in English as devised by the Curriculum Development Centre is at the moment serving the interests of a very small minority of children in the primary schools' (cf. Sharma, 1973). In the same year the results of the first CDC evaluation were made available as part of a former director's doctoral thesis (cf. McAdam, 1973). McAdam set out to compare the performance in a variety of tests of children who had gone through the newly introduced English-medium programme and those who had followed the conventional vernacular-medium programme. Not surprisingly, it was found that on average the children who had followed the new English-medium programme performed much better in tests of English language proficiency than those who had followed the older programme. It was also found that the English-medium group performed much better in social science tests conducted in English.[4] They were significantly worse, however, in mathematics, and particularly in problem arithmetic.[5] A significantly large minority of the English-medium group, furthermore, were found to be virtually illiterate, which is just what Sharma had found in his earlier study, which focused directly on reading.

Since the secondary schools cream off the top 15 per cent of the primary school leavers,[6] it might be expected that, whatever the general standard, the language skills of this selected group would be sufficiently well developed to meet the language requirements of the secondary-school curriculum. In fact, however, the written English of the secondary-school intake is considered to be so far below the minimum standard required that a remedial composition course, covering the most basic aspects of written composition, has been built into the junior secondry-school programme. The structural component of the course, furthermore, more or less duplicates the structural component of the primary school course. Despite this initial remedial effort, however, and the continuing attention paid throughout the junior secondary school to writing skills, there remains a significant qualitative gap between the kind of expositional writing skills required by the content subjects and the writing skills that English as a subject is able to develop.

As a subject, English is severely handicapped at the secondary level by the fact that it does not have any content matter of its own to exploit. Topics chosen in the English lessons for free composition tend to be topics relating to the everyday experience of the pupils which can be dealt with quite adequately by means of a simple narrative. Much of the compositional work done in class, furthermore, continues to be controlled and guided and focuses upon grammatical form and vocabulary rather than upon rhetorical devices and the organization of discourse. In practice, therefore, the compositional component of the course is little more than an extension or application of the structural component.

At the secondary level there is no commitment, even in principle, to an intergrated curriculum. Each subject is rigidly compartmentalized and taught by a specialist teacher who is unlikely to have any clear idea of what is being taught in more than one other subject. The system, therefore, does not encourage teachers of English to draw upon the content of other subjects for the purpose of developing basic expositional skills. There remains the possibility of extending the teaching of literature in the secondary schools as a means of providing English with some content of its own. As it is currently taught at the senior secondary level, however, literature tends to be just as rigidly compartmentalized as other subjects and can hardly be said to serve as an ancillary subject to English language.[7]

The gap as measured in terms of expositional skills, already wide at the senior secondary level, continues to widen at the tertiary level, and particularly at the university. At the same time a serious comprehension gap opens up as students find themselves abruptly faced with authentic academic texts in their area of specialization (cf. Wingard, 1971). Since in many cases the students cannot read their prescribed texts with adequate understanding, the texts do not serve the purpose they should as models of expositional or argumentational writing.

As a subject at university level, English has shown an increasing tendency in recent years to become equated with either English literature or general linguistics. In danger now of being overburdened with its own content, it is unable to service its own language needs, much less those of other subjects which continue to need linguistic support (cf. Wingard, *op. cit.*). Many students find themselves struggling to express concepts that are only dimly understood in a language which is quite inadequate for their needs. The result, all too often, is garbled and incoherent discourse devoid of any discernible sense. The following fragment of an essay on a linguistics topic is offered merely as an illustration of the kind of logically incoherent discourse that is commonly produced under examination conditions, even at third- or fourth-year level:

> Syntactic structure looks at the word order of language. It determines the use of words in correct and grammatical syntactic structure. In order for a sentence to be meaningful there has to be correct syntactic structure of words. Syntactic structure is greatly influenced by grammatical and lexical words which determine how they are placed in correct word order.

As a manifestation of the linguistic competence of a student approaching the terminal point of the educational system, this piece of nonsense discourse undoubtedly gives cause for concern. A careful examination of the language of the extract, however, reveals that the syntax is on the whole fairly sound. The student's problem, it would seem, is primarily a conceptual problem, which is arguably attributable to an English-medium policy which from the very beginning of the educational system has tended to encourage rote learning without cognition. Whatever the cause, deep-rooted conceptual problems cannot be solved overnight by intensive EAP courses of the kind currently offered in many other universities. The solutions, if they can be found, lie much further back in the educational system.

To sum up briefly at this point, all the available evidence points to the fact that as a subject English is failing to develop the degree of operational competence in the language that its use as a medium requires. The communication problem, it would appear, has its roots at the primary level, where the rigid structural syllabus gives little encouragement to the development of creative language skills. Since the pupils' communicative skills are underdeveloped, very little communicative interaction between teacher and pupils takes place inside the classroom. Children dutifully mime adult concepts but do not have sufficient control over the medium of learning to contribute, as they should, to their own conceptual growth.

2. Towards a new ELT strategy for Zambia

Now that the medium issue has been settled, at least for the foreseeable future, the Curriculum Development Centre is at last able to turn its attention to the long-standing need for an overall review of the existing English language programmes. The long-awaited official CDC evaluation of the primary course is already under way and preliminary findings indicate, predictably, that the course is failing to teach children to write correctly and coherently. Since the junior secondary-school course is now believed to be about right, no major evaluation exercise is planned for this level, but steps are being taken to develop the existing syllabus by the introduction of a further study skills component and an oral component with a communicative bias. The effectiveness of the senior secondary-school course in developing the kind of language skills needed in various categories of employment and for further study in tertiary institutions is, however, being assessed with a view to producing a common senior secondary-school syllabus.

Although there will no doubt be some modification and development of existing English language programmes as a result of the current spate of evaluation exercises, it seems unlikely that there will be any radical reappraisal of objectives and strategies. It seems to me, however, that the formidable case that has been built up over a number of years against the English-medium scheme (cf. Kapwepwe, 1970; Mphahlele, 1970; Kashoki, 1973; Serpell, 1978; Chishimba, 1979; Chishimba, 1980; Ngalube, 1981) cannot be countered by a mere cosmetic operation. What is needed now is nothing less than a thoroughgoing review of the implementation of the English-medium policy, and such a review, I would suggest, should be based not only on an evaluation of the existing courses from an internal perspective but also upon a consideration of alternative ELT strategies compatible with the Education Reform proposals (cf. Zambia Ministry of Education, 1977).

In this section I propose to identify and discuss a number of strategy options that seem to me to be potentially viable in the Zambian context. Although the options will be considered separately and independently of each other, they need not be viewed as global options nor as being mutually incompatible. Conditions in Zambia do not favour global solutions: language backgrounds, language needs and language-teaching resources vary too much from one part of the country to another and, indeed, within the same part of the country from one school to another. By isolating each of the options, however, it will be possible to reveal more clearly their merits and limitations.

2.1   The remedial option

I consider this option first because the junior secondary-school course, which from many points of view is the most satisfactory part of the present ELT programme in Zambia, is already to a large extent implicitly remedial. A remedial approach can be defended under the present circumstances, of course, on the grounds of practical necessity; it can also be defended in principle, however, as being an appropriate strategy for English as a subject in an English-medium context, although arguably the remedial process should begin much earlier in the system than it does in Zambia.
The case for a remedial strategy for English as a subject would rest on the claim that beyond the initial threshold level any further development of the pupils' competence in English is more likely to take place in the content subject lessons than in the English lessons, where, so the argument would

run, much of the teaching is redundant. There is no doubt that a good deal of vocabulary building does take place in the content subject lessons. It is also true that in practice many of the speech patterns in the primary and junior secondary-school syllabuses are introduced and used in the content subject lessons before they are taught in the English lessons, rather than the other way round as was originally intended. A principled remedial strategy would recognize and accept this state of affairs as being unavoidable and, indeed, desirable and assign to English as a subject the role of monitoring the linguistic development of the pupils with a view to ensuring that deviant features in their interlanguage are not allowed to consolidate and fossilize. It must be emphasized, however, that for such a strategy to be viable, content subject teachers would need to make a more systematic contribution to the teaching of English than they do at the present time in Zambia.

2.2   The communicative option

The current trend towards a more communicative approach in foreign-language teaching is beginning to influence ELT thinking in Zambia. In view of what was said earlier about the lack of classroom interaction between teacher and pupils, there would seem to be a strong case for a communicative bias in the English-language syllabuses, particularly at the primary level. I would like to suggest, however, that an out-and-out communicative approach to the teaching of English as a subject in the Zambian English-medium context may not only be unncessary but may also have undesirable and largely irremediable long-term consequences.

Although at the present time English is taught throughout most of the school system essentially as a foreign language in accordance with a conventional structural syllabus, it would be wrong to assume that at any given stage in the primary or junior secondary-school programme pupils have at their disposal only a partial and fragmentary linguistic system incapable of serving any real communicative needs. Because English is used to some extent as a medium of communication outside the classroom and as the medium of instruction inside the classroom, Zambian children, particularly those living in urban areas, activate and make use of what fragmentary knowledge of the language they have from a very early stage, and as they begin to use the language they develop it in accordance with hypotheses they themselves form on the basis of the data they are exposed to (cf. Nemser, 1971). What eventually emerges is a functional interlanguage (cf. Selinker, 1972 and Simukoko, 1979), which gradually approximates to the more mature, though in many cases far from fully developed, language of the teacher. In such a situation, and indeed in ESL situations generally, there is less need to adopt a communicative approach to the teaching of English as a subject than there would be in a typical EFL situation in which English is not normally used as a means of communication in the everyday environment of the learner.

A danger inherent in a situation which encourages the premature use of an interlanguage for real communicative purposes, however, is that the interlanguage will stabilize and gradually fossilize at the point where it minimally meets the communicative demands placed upon it. If fossilization takes place on a wide scale, there may be an irreversible drift towards creolization.[8] Indeed, some observers believe that a hybrid variety of English ('Zamblish') is already beginning to emerge in Zambia (cf. Haynes, 1981). I shall have a little more to say about creolization as a possible strategy option presently. At this juncture, I wish merely to draw attention to the fact that an out-and-out communicative approach in the teaching of English in the schools, by encouraging use at the expense of correct usage, may have the effect of accelerating the process of creolization.

2.3   The simplification option

The rationale underlying the simplification option is that it would narrow the linguistic gap between the interlanguage of the pupils and the medium of instruction by approximating the medium to the interlanguage without encouraging grammatical deviation. Although some degree of simplification is now an accepted feature of foreign-language teaching, however, it seems doubtful that simplification can be upheld as a viable overriding strategy in an ESL situation.

As it was originally conceived, the Zambian primary course was intended to be a linguistically integrated course in which the readability not only of the supplementary readers but also that of the course books in other subjects would be adjusted so as to conform with the grade levels specified in the English syllabus. The integration project failed primarily because writers of course books in other subjects refused to accept the linguistic constraints imposed by the English Medium Centre. The Permanent Secretary for Education at the time, Mr Mulikita, warned against the danger of English-language specialists at the Centre setting themselves up as adjudicators of course material written for subjects other than English (cf. Higgs, *op. cit.*). He quite sensibly upheld the view that competent writers will endeavour to make the subject matter they are presenting as accessible as possible to their intended readership and that linguistic censorship may impede rather than facilitate learning in the long run.[9]

Although it is by no means certain that it would facilitate learning, some degree of linguistic simplification of the textbooks and course material in use in Zambian schools would no doubt be feasible enough. Much less feasible, and probably even less desirable, would be the simplification of the oral exposition of the teacher in the classroom. Chishimba (1980) has given us an interesting illustration of the kind of problems a primary-school teacher faces when trying to present an introductory lesson on the life cycle of a butterfly in controlled English. The teacher, he points out, has to be worried about every item of vocabulary and structure, about sentence length and complexity, and about pronunciation and spelling, as well as about the content and organization of the lesson. The result is likely to be incoherent and fragmented discourse which may well be less intelligible to the pupils than a linguistically uncontrolled exposition would be. To achieve simplification in English without loss of coherence and without distortion of the content requires a degree of proficiency and articulateness in the language far higher than that possessed by the average Zambian primary-school teacher. As a teaching strategy, therefore, simplification is not only questionable in principle but extremely difficult to implement in practice.

It may be argued, furthermore, that by deliberately simplifying the medium so that it approximates more closely to the interlanguage of the pupils, teachers would deprive their pupils of a satisfactory model of English in use and thereby encourage the drift towards creolization that I spoke of earlier. Some educationalists in Zambia view this drift with equanimity, regarding it as a natural process that should not be interfered with (cf. Haynes, *op. cit.*). As an educational policy option, however, creolization has little to recommend it. It would encourage not only the simplification but also the grammatical distortion of the medium and conceivably impoverish it to such an extent that it would no longer satisfactorily serve as a medium for the exposition of basic concepts and arguments in the essential core subjects (cf. Herriott, 1971: 42–43, for further discussion on this matter).

2.4 The ESP option

Although English is used to a limited extent in the urban areas as a lingua franca, it is primarily needed for educational and occupational purposes. A prima facie case could be made out, therefore, for an English programme which, beyond the elementary stages, gradually acquires a strong ESP bias. If such a programme were developed, English as a subject, far from laying claim to a position of primacy within the curriculum, would assume a more supportive role as a service subject for the English-medium content subjects. As such, it would in effect cease to exist as an independent subject and would be taught, somewhat in the manner suggested by Allen and Widdowson (1974), as an aspect of other subjects.

Although this option has much to recommend it, however, it would be difficult to implement satisfactorily in the Zambian context. At the primary level, teachers of English are also teachers of most if not all other subjects in the curriculum. When they teach English they know just what is being taught at the corresponding grade levels in the other subjects and may be expected, therefore, to have some idea of what the linguistic requirements of the other subjects are. The situation at the secondary level, however, where an ESP bias would be more appropriate, is entirely different. The teaching is more narrowly specialized and teachers of English are unlikely to have much familiarity with the content of other subjects being taught. Any *ad hoc* ESP teaching at the secondary level, therefore, would have to involve a degree of co-operation between the English teacher and the content subject teachers that would be difficult to promote in practice.

As for the design of a completely new ESP syllabus for use in Zambian secondary schools, to be effective this would have to be backed up with tailor-made course material. The mere provision of teachers' handbooks recommending an ESP approach and providing an outline syllabus would not be enough, for few if any of the teachers have any valid ESP experience other than that which they have gained working with the reading skills component of the junior secondary-school course. Nor is there much relevant knowledge or experience they could draw upon indirectly. Very little is known in general terms about the language of school textbooks or about the expositional registers used by classroom teachers in the different subject areas (see, however, Edwards, 1976: 148 et seq.). Pieces of text could of course be extrapolated from the various textbooks in use in the schools, but the mere collection of a body of texts would not in itself serve any useful purpose if the teachers do not know what to do with them. The work that has been done elsewhere in the ESP field has been mainly with academically advanced students who have already acquired, through the medium of their mother-tongue, a good deal of knowledge and understanding of their subject —knowledge and understanding, incidentally, which might profitably be exploited in an ESP programme (cf. Widdowson, *op. cit.*: 44 et seq.). The problem, consequently, has not generally been perceived as being one of getting the basic content matter of a range of different subjects across (which is what it is in Zambia) but rather one of equipping students with a second language as an auxiliary tool in a particular area of specialization.

Whatever the arguments for a stronger ESP bias in the English programmes, therefore, it would be unrealistic to expect any systematic ESP programmes to be developed by the Curriculum Development Centre. Under present circumstances, a more realistic expectation might be that the content subject teachers themselves could be encouraged to accept more responsibility for the teaching of English for their own special purposes. They, far better than the English teachers, know what the language needs of the pupils are in their respective subject areas.

2.5   The integration option

If English is to be effectively taught as an aspect of other subjects, then arguably it should not be merely correlated with other subjects in the curriculum but fully integrated with them. An integration strategy would require that all teachers in English become effective teachers of English through the teaching of subjects other than English. Of course, not all subjects have the same potential for exploitation for language-teaching purposes. One would not expect mathematics, for example, to make precisely the same contribution to the pupils' linguistic development as, say, history. The nature of the contribution that a subject might be expected to make would depend partly upon the nature of its content matter and partly upon its intrinsic methodology.

The implementation of an integration strategy and the consequent abandonment of English as a subject would involve a radical shift away from a language-teaching methodology which presents language as an inventory of forms and structures to be taught in sequence and in isolation towards a methodology which presents language as coherent and meaningful discourse (cf. Widdowson, *op. cit.*: 248). It would involve, in other words, a shift from an analytical approach better suited to an EFL situation to a synthetic approach better suited to an ESL situation. There is no reason in principle, however, why recurring forms and structures which the exposition of a subject requires but which prove persistently troublesome for the pupils should not be isolated and practised in the traditional way.

Although there is nothing new in either the idea or the practice of teaching English language by way of teaching some other subject (cf. Bullock, 1975; Lee, 1975; Bernstein, 1977; Widdowson, 1968 and 1979; Moorhouse, 1980, etc.), any attempt to integrate English language teaching with the teaching of other subjects in Zambian schools would require a fundamental change of thinking and attitude on the part of both policy-makers and ordinary classroom teachers. Not only would the cherished idea of a fixed syllabus for English have to be abandoned, and with it the fruits of years of productive effort by the Curriculum Development Centre, but a radical change in teacher-pupil roles and relationships inside the classroom would have to be brought about. Teachers in all subject areas would need to adopt a more communicative approach to the teaching subject, and such an approach would have to involve a good deal more interaction and creative dialogue between teacher and pupils than normally takes place at the present time in Zambian classrooms.

3. Concluding remarks

Although a case could be made out in principle for each of the options discussed in the foregoing section, none of them can be seriously entertained as a panacea for all the ills induced by the English-medium policy. Nor does the remedy seem to lie in the adoption of a well-balanced eclectic approach incorporating elements of each of the alternative strategies. What is called for in the Zambian situation, I would like to suggest, is a more flexible and less prescriptive approach which permits teachers to slant existing courses in any one of the directions suggested by the different strategy options we have considered, in such a way as to make the courses more relevant to local needs and more compatible with local resources.

At the same time, however, it needs to be recognized that there are limits to what English as a subject can do. The failure of the English-medium policy to achieve its primary objective of facilitating learning may be attributed as much to a misguided integration strategy based on the primacy of English as a subject as to any inadequacies in the English courses themselves. This strategy was abandoned with the dismantling of the English Medium Centre and its replacement by the Curriculum Development Centre, but regrettably the strategy has not been superseded by a more viable and more enlightened strategy which recognizes the mutual dependency and complementarity of English as a subject and English as a medium. Until we know much more than we do at present about how each individual subject can best contribute to the teaching of English, however, there is little that the Curriculum Development Centre can do to promote an integrative approach by way of syllabus design. The task of upgrading English language teaching in Zambia would seem to devolve, then, upon the teacher training institutions. Teacher trainers, at all levels, need to cultivate in their students an awareness and understanding not only of the crucial importance of language skills in the learning process but also of the complementary roles that English as a subject and English as a medium have to play in developing those skills. How best to exploit this complementarity is not a question to which there are any ready-made answers, but unless the question is addressed in the teacher training centres, it seems unlikely that the level of competence in English needed to facilitate early concept formation will ever be achieved.

Notes

1. The original decision to adopt a universal English-medium policy was defended by the Minister of Education at the time, Mr John Mwanakatwe, on the grounds that it would both improve the pupils' skills in English and facilitate learning in other subjects (cf. Mwanakatwe, 1968: 215). This assumption appears to have been based on Lenneberg's claim that there is a critical age — about 12 — beyond which children cannot acquire native-speaker competence in a language (cf. Lenneberg, 1967 and Chishimba, 1980).
2. For well-researched accounts of the historical background to this decision, see Higgs (1980) and Shana (1980).
3. Hugh Africa (1980) reports the results of a comparison of the performance of Zambian primary and secondary school children on the IEA tests with the performance of comparable sets of children in various other countries where English is taught and used as a foreign language only. The results show that the level of achievement in English of Zambian school children, despite the advantage of an English-medium context, is not superior in the listening, speaking and writing skills. Zambian children achieved higher scores only on the reading comprehension test.
4. Reservations have been expressed about these findings, however (cf. Zambia Ministry of Education, 1975).
5. A further study carried out in 1974 on Grade 3 numeracy in English-medium classes revealed very poor learning performance, which the researchers ascribed to the use of a non-indigenous language as the medium of instruction (cf. Sharma and Henderson, 1974). This finding was reinforced by a survey carried out in Ghana (cf. Omani Collison, 1975), which was reported by an Evaluation Committee set up by the Ministry of Education to examine the impact of English medium on children's learning (cf. Zambia Ministry of Education, 1975). The Evaluation Committee came out strongly against the English-medium policy.
6. Selection for secondary education is based on a wide range of tests but the criterion which seems to work best in predicting future all-round success at the secondary-school level is proficiency in English (cf. Sharma, 1974).
7. For some ideas on how literature in Zambian schools might be exploited for linguistic purposes, see Moody (1981).
8. Richards (1972) has shown that many similarities exist between creoles and interlanguage.

9. The point has been made elsewhere (cf. Widdowson, 1979: 192 et seq.) that the simplification of the syntax and lexis of a piece of text does not necessarily make the propositional content any more accessible. It may, indeed, obscure it by interfering with the coherence of the text.

References

AFRICA, HUGH (1980) Language in education in a multilingual state. Unpublished PhD thesis, University of Toronto.

ALLEN, J. P. B. and WIDDOWSON, H. G. (1974) Teaching the communicative use of English. In: *IRAL*, Vol. XII.

BERNSTEIN, B. (1977) *Class, Codes, and Control.* Vol. 3: *Towards a Theory of Educational Transmissions.* Routledge, London.

BULLOCK, A. (1975) *A Language for Life* (The Bullock Report). HMSO, London.

CHISHIMBA, C. P. (1979) A study of the Zambia primary English course. Unpublished PhD thesis, Columbia University.

CHISHIMBA, M. M. (1980) Observations on the English medium component of the Zambia primary course. In: *Zambia Educational Review*, Vol. 2.

EDWARDS, A. D. (1981) *Language in Culture and Class.* Heinemann, London.

HAYNES, R. (1981) The emergence of an English-based creole in Zambia: possibilities and implications. Unpublished paper, University of Zambia.

HERRIOTT, P. (1971) *Language and Teaching: a Psychological View.* Methuen, London.

HIGGS, P. L. (1980) The introduction of English as the medium of instruction in Zambian schools. In: *Zambia Educational Review*, Vol. 2.

KAPWEPWE, S. M. (1970) Closing address. In: *Report on the First National Educational Conference.* Government Printers, Lusaka.

KASHOKI, M. E. (1973) Language: a blueprint for national integration? In: *Bulletin of the Zambia Language Group*, Vol. 6.

LEE, M. (1975) *Integrating ESL with other subjects.* ATEFL pamphlet.

LENNEBERG, E. (1967) *Biological Foundations of Language.* John Wiley, New York.

McADAM, B. H. G. (1973) The effectiveness of the new English medium primary school curriculum in Zambia. Unpublished PhD thesis, Manchester University.

MOODY, J. (1981) Some comments on how literature might be exploited for linguistic purposes. Unpublished paper, University of Zambia.

MOORHOUSE, C. (1980) Linked-skills courses: an account of the theory and methodology of linking literacy teaching with specialist subject areas. In: *Teacher Training in ESP* (ELT Documents 106). ETIC, London.

MPHAHLELE, E. (1970) Some thoughts on culture in Zambia. In: *The Jewel of Africa*, Vol. 2.

MWANAKATWE, J. (1968) *The Growth of Education in Zambia.* Longman, London.

NGALUBE, J. H. (1981) Some thoughts about the place of English in our education system. In: *The English Teachers Journal*, Vol. 5. The English Teachers Association of Zambia, Lusaka.

NEMSER, W. (1971) Approximative systems of foreign language learners. In: *IRAL*, Vol. IX.

OMANI COLLISON, G. (1975) Concept formation in a second language. In: *Harvard Educational Review*, Vol. XLIV.

RICHARDS, J. C. (1972) Social factors, interlanguage, and language learning. In: *Language Learning*, Vol. 22.

SELINKER, L. (1972) *Interlanguage.* In: *IRAL*, Vol. X.

SERPELL, R. (1978) Some developments in Zambia since 1971. In: OHANESSIAN, S. and KASHOKI, M. E. (eds.), *Language in Zambia.* International African Institute, London.

SERPELL, R. (1981) The cultural context of language learning. In: *The English Teachers Journal*, Vol. 5. The English Teachers Association of Zambia, Lusaka.

SHANA, S. C. G. (1980) Which language? A brief history of the medium of instruction issue in Northern Rhodesia. In: *Zambia Educational Review*, Vol. 2.

SHARMA, R. (1973) *The Reading Skills of Grade 3 Children.* Ministry of Education, Lusaka.

SHARMA, R. (1974) *The Grade 7 Composite Examination: a critique* (Psychological Services Report No. 2). Ministry of Education, Lusaka.

SHARMA, R. and HENDERSON, T. (1974) *Numeracy at the Grade 3 Level.* Ministry of Education, Lusaka.

SIMUKOKO, Y. T. (1979) Second language learning and description: a theoretical frame of reference for studying Zambian English. In: *Bulletin of the Zambia Languages Group*, Vol. 4.

WIDDOWSON, H. G. (1968) The teaching of English through science. In: DAKIN, J., TIFFEN, B. and WIDDOWSON, H. G. *Language in Education.* OUP, London.

WIDDOWSON, H. G. (1979) *Explorations in Applied Linguistics.* OUP, London.

WINGARD, P. (1971) English for scientists at the University of Zambia. In: *CILT Reports and Papers* No. 7.

ZAMBIA MINISTRY OF EDUCATION (1975) *The Impact of English Medium on Children's Learning.* Evaluation Committee Report. Ministry of Education, Lusaka.

ZAMBIA MINISTRY OF EDUCATION (1977) *Educational Reform: Proposals and Recommendations.* Government Printers, Lusaka.

PLANNING A PROJECT: THE KELT PROJECT, SIERRA LEONE

ANN HAYES

Ministry of Education, Sierra Leone

Introduction

One of the principal tenets of policy underlying the Key English Language Teaching scheme (hereafter referred to as KELT) is projectization. There are many KELT posts in Africa, as well as in other parts of the world; ELT experts recruited for jobs in Ministries, universities, or teacher-training institutions, where they beaver away at curriculum development, syllabus design, materials production, pre- and in-service teacher education, and all the other aspects of work they can be confronted with as advisers, lecturers or whatever. There have until recently, however, been very few KELT operations based, as the word 'project' implies, on thorough and thoughtful planning, with clear objectives open to evaluation at any stage, and detailed implementation schemes with realistic time-scales. This state of affairs is, like most other things in life, directly attributable to nothing and no one in particular: it is partly a result of old schemes (e.g. the non-project-based ACE, Aid to Commonwealth English, and BESS, British Expatriate Supplementation Scheme) merging slowly and painfully with new ones; partly an indication of the inherent difficulty in spotting potential projects and effectively setting them up from British Council Headquarters, local representations, or, for that matter, any vantage-point outside the local education system; partly a reminder of what can so often happen to the best-laid plans of mice and men.

We were lucky in Sierra Leone. We arrived on reasonably virgin soil as far as British ELT assistance was concerned; a couple of BESS English Literature lecturers at the university, a handful of VSOs teaching English at secondary level, an occasional whispered mention in the odd corner of some British Council English Language Officer or other who had passed that way, or held a seminar, or presented some books, in the early seventies, or the mid-sixties, or even more bygone days. There was, therefore, nothing and no one in particular to incorporate under our brief (more of which, later). We could start from scratch.

We had, moreover, both the time and the opportunity to plan, in that one post, the central co-ordinating post based in the Ministry of Education, was filled a year ahead of the others. This meant sufficient time to acquire a

15

thoroughgoing knowledge of the Sierra Leonean educational system from the inside, and the opportunity to devise detailed plans and schemes for the project using that knowledge.

Finally, we were given scope and leeway to plan in that our original brief, involving teacher-training for primary level English, was clearly stated, yet flexible enough to allow for a bit of reinterpretation here and there. The team of project designers from the British Council's English Language Division in London, who had come to Sierra Leone for a couple of weeks and put together, with the aid of the local representation, some project objectives and job specifications, had couched these in terms sufficiently general to permit further modifications and adaptations. They were wise enough not to specify the project so tightly as to strangle its potential, and wise enough to listen to reason when alterations to their original specifications were suggested in the light of a deeper and further-reading knowledge of the situation than their brief time in-country could possibly have afforded them.

And so, by September 1980, KELT had come to Sierra Leone. Wise mentors, a clean slate, time for thought and planning. Not a bad start for any project. As I said, we were lucky.

But luck itself is not everything. Hard work and common sense count for a lot too, even more so perhaps at the initial stages of planning and setting up a project. The hard work here comprises finding the answers to a lot of questions; the common sense lies in knowing which questions to ask, and where the answers are most likely to be found. Our planning process, therefore, followed a question-and-answer pattern as follows:

1. Why are we here in Sierra Leone?

The immediate answer is because the Sierra Leone government has been acutely aware of falling standards in English for some time now, and is seeking help to 'revitalize English language teaching at primary level' (as the original job specifications put it). The most effective help is considered to be in the form of teacher-training, with as much input as possible at pre-service level to the five primary teacher training colleges in the country, and at in-service level for the 7500 strong body of serving primary-school teachers, over 60 per cent of whom are unqualified and untrained, many of whom are, in fact, only about one jump ahead of the children they purport to teach.

Observation of English classes in many different schools in different parts of the country indeed tells us that ELT is ailing and in need of revitalization. The symptoms are all too familiar: teacher-centred work with the children getting little opportunity to practise their own English; the meaningless noise of endless repetition and reading aloud with no real understanding of the language being used; an over formal grammar-based approach which presents English as a dead language rather than a vital medium of communication; an inability to hit the right level of teaching, with the children in many areas of work being asked to do too much for their abilities and age, and in others too little to stretch or interest them. These symptoms can be directly traced to a number of causes: the 1969 Trial Syllabus in official use in the schools is more of a general guideline for the teaching of English in Sierra Leone than a proper detailed syllabus teachers can refer to for everyday use; the Selective Entrance examination for secondary level, in traditional grammar-and-vocabulary-questions mould, has an immense backwash effect on teaching in the upper primary classes, yet bears no relation whatsoever to the 1969 Trial Syllabus mentioned above; the African languages — the first, and sometimes second as well — languages of the school children, are given no official recognition in the syllabus and no meaningful role in the teaching of English; the teacher-training system suffers from a teachers' certificate syllabus as vague and inadequate as the school syllabus, a lack of effective in-service training schemes, and a general preoccupation with the theoretical, academic side of ELT rather than the more practical aspects which could be put to immediate use in the school classroom.

Following from the above diagnosis, the remedy would seem to be fairly clear. What we need is

- a syllabus for the schools,
- materials to realise the syllabus,
- a new Selective Entrance examination to reflect the syllabus,
- a TC syllabus to prepare teachers in training for the above,
- an in-service scheme to prepare serving teachers to the same end.

All very laudable aims for ODA-recruited practitioners of English-language teaching working in key posts in the Ministry and teachers' colleges. All very KELT-worthy, in fact.

But a closer examination of the situation reveals that most of the ingredients for a remedy are all to hand:

- The preparatory phase of the Third IDA/Sierra Leone Government Education Project, focusing on primary education, is just getting under way, and one of its principal aims is curriculum development, involving preparation of new syllabi for the main subjects, including English, and provision of basic materials based on these syllabi to the schools.
- Teachers' college English departments with many bright, well-qualified, enthusiastic members of staff, work to a syllabus set by a chief examiner and advisory board based on the Institute of Education in Freetown, but incorporating their own modifications.
- An in-service training scheme, funded by the EEC, operates annual one-week courses over a five-year period, to cover all main primary-level subjects, for unqualified teachers in various parts of the country drawing on local schools and colleges for staff, and working to a syllabus derived from the teachers' college syllabus.

— Inspectorate staff, inspectors and teacher-supervisors, in their own districts, and headteachers in their schools, work with admirable dedication, in difficult and often demoralizing conditions, to help teachers and maintain standards.

— A remarkable quantity and quality of educational expertise exists in the schools, in the Ministry of Education, in the teacher-training colleges, in the Institute of Education, in the University colleges.

The basic elements to remedy the situation are all there. KELT assistance would seem to be superfluous, until even closer inspection of the situation reveals that these elements are disparate and static. They need a dynamic and cohesive agent in order to become effective. The Sierra Leoneans have the professional expertise to remedy the ELT situation by themselves. They have a framework whereby the remedy can be administered. What they lack is the co-ordination required to effect its administration. There is no real link-up, no consistency in all that is going on in primary-level ELT — curriculum development, materials production, test design, pre-service and in-service teacher-training. As in so many typically aid-worthy contexts, there is plenty going on, projects galore, but precious little co-ordination between them all. The aims of the KELT project therefore become clearer: support and co-ordination. No point in starting up yet another independent project. No point in further confusing the poor Ministry of Education, which can scarcely keep tabs on all the educational projects in progress as it is. Better to take what already exists, what is already under way, and try to render it more effective. At long last we have the answer to our question: we are here to help the Sierra Leoneans in what they are already doing in ELT and to co-ordinate their efforts. And from this point on, all the other questions and answers fall into place much more easily.

2. What can we do to achieve our aims?

Our general aim of fulfilling a supportive and co-ordinating role can be realized through meeting three basic objectives:

— Helping the Sierra Leoneans produce and implement a new primary English syllabus and materials to realize it in the schools within the framework of the Third IDA Education Project. This objective is the crucial one, since although the original KELT brief is teacher-training, we must have something to teacher-train for, a focus for both pre-service and in-service work which the present inadequate school syllabus and woefully lacking school textbooks cannot provide.

— Co-ordinating the English departments of the primary teacher-training colleges, along with the chief examiners for the teachers' certificate, to produce a new TC syllabus based upon the new school syllabus, thus ensuring that teachers are produced from the colleges able to cope straightaway with the teaching situation in the schools.

— Ensuring that in-service work carried out by Ministry staff, inspectors and teacher-supervisors, and by staff of the EEC-funded short courses, i.e. TC lecturers, primary headteachers, secondary-school teachers and members of the inspectorate, supports the new school syllabus and is in tune with pre-service work, involving a close liaison between Ministry officials, TC staff and school teachers.

— Alerting the relevant West African Examinations Council authorities to what is happening in primary English with a view to modifying the Selective Entrance exam in the light of the new school syllabus, and likewise alerting the secondary system to the changes to come so they can accommodate them in their own school and teacher-training syllabi.

'Helping', 'co-ordinating', 'ensuring', 'alerting'. Perhaps none of these objectives sound as solid and concrete as 'producing', 'preparing', or 'writing' would. But how many syllabi have been produced by expatriate 'experts' and left to yellow in a drawer of some Ministry official? How many textbooks have been written by the same to remain unpublished and forgotten in some British Council archive, never to see the light of day in the country they were written for? We must recognize not only the Sierra Leonean strengths and weaknesses, but also our own in the Sierra Leonean situation. Better to help them apply the remedy they want, than simply offer the remedy we think they should have.

3.   Who will do all this?

Obviously suitably qualified and experienced ELT practitioners recruited by the British Council to work in ODA-funded posts designated as key ELT posts by the Sierra Leone Government. But a handful of KELTs (and funds will only permit a handful, especially in a country as small as this), however conscientious and hardworking, cannot hope to achieve by themselves such wide-ranging, nationally applicable objectives as are outlined above. They need help and support. So, we look around and see that another British input to ELT in Sierra Leone comes from VSO. They have a number of volunteers teaching English in secondary schools, but are becoming somewhat disgruntled about the effectiveness of these posts, and therefore react with enthusiasm to the suggestion that they might instead make their major contribution to ELT in Sierra Leone through our primary project.

We continue to look around, beyond purely British inputs to ELT, but find that there are none in terms of personnel. The Americans distribute Forum, but no longer even have the annual visit of a peripatetic TESOL expert. Peace Corps make their main contribution to primary education in the fields of maths and science and only incidentally touch on language teaching. The Australians give a few awards each year for Sierra Leoneans to do ELT courses in Australia. The EEC provides funds for in-service courses, but leaves staffing and professional input entirely to Sierra Leoneans.

And so, in manpower terms, the field is narrowed. It comes down to KELTS,

VSOs and, of course, Sierra Leoneans, both trained and trainable, both actual and potential contributors to primary-level ELT in their country.

4. Where will they do it?

The next step is to take the available manpower and see where it can be used to best effect in meeting the objectives. This involves setting up a framework, a co-ordinating mechanism which will provide for control and co-ordination of ELT in all parts of the country and at all levels of the primary education system. A tall order, but in a country as small as Sierra Leone (total population about three and a half million), not an impossible one.

Two vital points must be borne in mind when constructing this framework: it must serve to link the teachers' colleges, responsible for pre-service teacher education, with the Ministry of Education inspectorate offices, responsible for in-service work and what actually happens in the schools; it must not collapse when the expatriate elements, the KELTS and VSOs, are withdrawn. With these two points in mind the task of drawing up construction plans can begin. We are basically concerned with teachers' colleges and Ministry of Education offices, and any decision on these must be based on an informed picture of how they operate in a national context.

FIG. 1

Sierra Leone is divided into three Provinces, North, South and East, and the comparatively tiny Western Area (Fig. 1). Of the five primary teachers' colleges in the country, two are located in the Northern Province, at Port Loko and Makeni, one in the Southern Province at Bo, one in the Eastern Province at Bunumbu, and one in the Western Area in Freetown. The Ministry of Education operates a policy of decentralization, with an education office in each provincial capital, Bo, Makeni and Kenema, under its own Regional Principal Education Officer, himself responsible to the Chief Education Officer in Freetown. In addition, each province and the five in the Northern Province (Kambia, Port Loko, Koinadugu, Bombali and Tonkolili), three in the Eastern Province (Kenema, Kono and Kailahun), and four in the Southern Province (Bo, Moyamba, Pujehun and Bonthe). Each of these districts, along with Western Area Rural and Western Area Urban, has its own Inspector of Schools, working, with a team of supervisors and teacher-supervisors, from an education office. Some of these teacher-supervisors specialize in one or two subjects (Western Area Urban, for example, has its own ELT teacher-supervisor, Australian-trained), but most are generalists. Their job entails helping teachers and maintaining standards through regular school visits in their districts, and through holding teacher-training workshops in different district zones.

The framework, then, is half-built for us. Most of the paths are already there for the infiltration of the KELT project. We need KELTs in the teachers' colleges, KELTs who will not only bring their experience and expertise to their particular college, but will also encourage liaison between colleges, and liaison between their particular college and their provincial education office. We need VSOs in district education offices, working at grass-roots level with teachers in the schools as teacher-supervisors for KELT. We need Sierra Leoneans in the teachers' colleges to work with the KELTs. We need Sierra Leoneans in both provincial and district-level education offices who, with a minimum of practical training or updating, could work with both KELTs and VSOs as teacher-supervisors for ELT. We need a KELT and one or two Sierra Leoneans in the Ministry of Education itself to supervise the whole programme and see that the necessary bureaucratic wheels are kept turning. We need in fact something like that seen in Fig. 2.

The actual framework finally decided upon does not correspond exactly to the one given above. As with most things, the practical lacks the beautiful symmetry of the ideal, and our final framework must take account of these important points:

— Bunumbu TC is the site of an ongoing UNESCO project aimed at training teachers specifically for rural areas. They are involved in curriculum development and syllabus design work of their own. While, therefore, Bunumbu TC English department must not be left out of the project, it would not seem right at this stage to place a KELT there. We must keep them informed of what we are doing, but not involve them fully, as a UNESCO pilot project, with what is essentially a national IDA/SLG project. With regard to KELT liaison with provincial

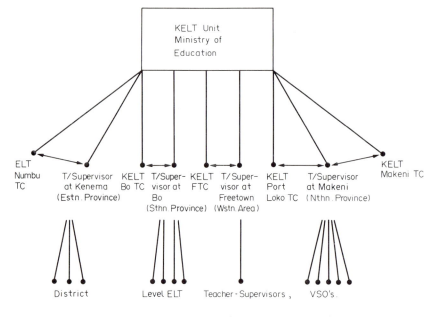

FIG. 2

education offices, Kenema, capital of the Eastern Province where Bunumbu is situated, is less than an hour's drive from Bo on a good road. KELT Bo can therefore serve it.

— Western Area is very small, largely urban (Freetown), and not considered especially VSO-worthy. Moreover, its schools are already fairly well serviced by central Ministry, urban and rural education office staff. VSO would prefer to concentrate its manpower on the provincial areas, where the material needs in the schools are greater, and the task of the inspectorate staff made harder by the distances to be covered, the number of schools to be visited, and their own paucity in number.

Our final framework therefore comes out as shown in Fig. 3.

Through various types of UK training under the Technical Co-operation Award Scheme and through working with KELTs and VSOs, identified counterparts should be gradually able to take over their roles, so that by the end of the project the framework will still stand, but be totally Sierra Leonean (see Fig. 4).

5. When will the work be done?

Any project must be realized within certain time-constraints, and ours are fairly clear. Our planning started in 1980. Books produced as part of the Third IDA Education Project are expected to go into the schools in 1983/84. KELT contracts are normally for two-year periods, renewable. VSOs usually

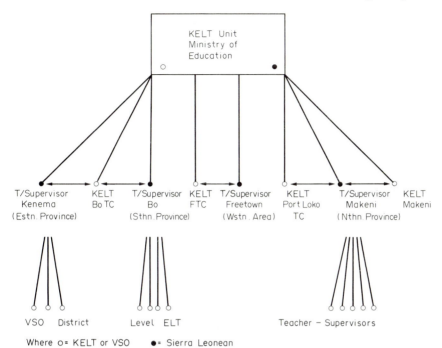

FIG. 3

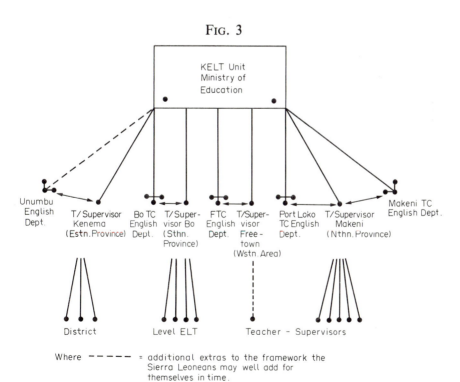

FIG. 4

stay at post for two years, with the option of an additional third year. Our time-scale can therefore realistically span a five-year period, from 1980 to 1985.

For the sake of simplicity, we can have two time-scales, one for setting up the project framework (see Fig. 5); and another for planning project activity in relation to the preparation and introduction of the new English syllabus and materials under the terms of the Third IDA Education Project:

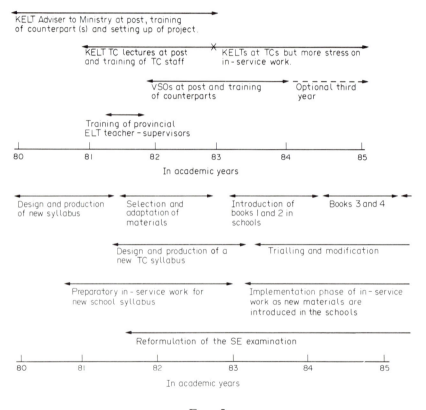

FIG. 5

As is made clear by these time-scales, the framework should be established and fully functioning by 1985, when the KELT project is due to end, but the activity should be ongoing, undertaken by the Sierra Leoneans working within the framework, and in no way affected by the departure of the KELTs and VSOs.

By this stage, we were ready to lay our plans before ODA and persuade them of their feasibility, given the required manpower and material support in terms of transport, tools of the trade, etc. We were convinced that our project had more than a chance of getting off the ground, based as it was on a thoroughgoing knowledge of the situation built up over months of school and teachers' college visits, of chats with Sierra Leoneans at all levels of the educational system, of attendance at all manner of educational meetings, both national and local. Moreover, we had based our planning on three principles we felt to be essential to any successful project:

— *Flexibility*. We tried not to strangle ourselves with our own project specifications, in the knowledge of what can so easily happen to the best-laid plans. Planning is an ongoing process in the life of any project, in that it must respond to the inevitable changes in the situation. Our priority is a strong framework which can cope with any necessary changes of activity as the years go on, which can respond to any new need, which can survive when the expatriates move out.
— *Humility*. We tried to build into our plans a recognition that the Sierra Leoneans know best when it comes to their own education system. The expatriate specialists are there to help the Sierra Leoneans do what they want to do, not to impose on them what they themselves think best.
— *Transferability*. We tried to design a project which would not collapse when the expatriates left, but could be handed over to and run by the Sierra Leoneans themselves. This involves identification of counterparts at all levels, appropriate UK training where and when necessary, the building of a framework incorporating both Sierra Leonean and KELT/VSO expertise.

Plans of any kind usually look grand on paper, and a readable, apparently feasible, clear plan can help to winkle funds from the tightest of purses and co-operation from the strictest of sources. But the proof of the plan lies in the implementing of it, and, in Sierra Leone, we are now only a few months into that phase. So far, so good with setting up the framework. . . .

KELT Unit, Ministry of Education. A clearly defined little unit exists within the Ministry, comprising KELT Adviser, an official counterpart, strong on the administrative side, and an unofficial counterpart, a teacher-supervisor, strong on professional ELT. The former is in the UK for a year's training (Dip. TEO) 1981–82, and the latter will go with four other teacher-supervisors for three months' practical training in the UK, April–June 1982.

KELT lecturers in the teachers' colleges. There are now four KELTs at post in Makeni, Port Loko, Freetown and Bo, each equipped with a landrover and an adequate travel allowance. Precise job descriptions, including teaching load, days off for observation of schools, liaison with the local inspectorate, in-service work etc. have been circulated to all concerned with their work, both in the colleges and education offices. Heads of their departments have already done a year's training in the UK (1980–81) and further counterparts have been identified for similar training in 1982–83.

ELT teacher-supervisors at provincial level. The Ministry has identified likely designates for these posts, some already teacher-supervisors in a general capacity, others headteachers who can be transferred after training to the provincial education offices. A party of five should be going to UK in April 1982 for three months' practical work on a specially tailored course and series of visits.

VSO teacher-supervisors at district level. The Ministry has approved the idea and made an official request to VSO. VSO is about to start the recruiting campaign, and we are at present involved in persuading ODA to provide motor-bikes and travel allowances for these posts to be effective.

An so far, so good with the activity.

IDA Project syllabus design and materials provision. This is so far going to plan. An English syllabus has been drawn up, by a largely Sierra Leonean panel with KELT membership, evaluated, and revised in the light of the evaluation. The syllabus is acceptable to the Ministry, and at present a tender document is being prepared for provision of materials to realize the syllabus in the schools.

Preparatory in-service work. A term of successful in-service work has been completed, bringing the philosophy and principles of the new syllabus to headteachers, inspectorate staff and TC English departments throughout the country. Planning for a second term is under way.

Producing a new TC syllabus. Planning meetings have been held at the Ministry, and it is hoped that a first all-TC meeting will be held in April 1982, with representatives from English departments in all the colleges, to commence work on a new syllabus. Money has been found to cover subsistence costs for four or five such meetings over the 1982–83 period, and KELTs will be responsible for their organization.

Selective Entrance Examination. The Research and Development Unit of the West African Examinations Council in Freetown has been alerted to the new syllabus developments and the subsequent need for modification of the present secondary entrance examination. The head of the unit will be attending a course on testing in the UK in June 1982, and thereafter it is hoped that closer liaison between him and the KELT project can be established and maintained.

But it has not all gone like clockwork, nor, indeed, can it be expected to do so in the future. At times, it has all seemed to be going rather anti-clockwise, and the problems have mainly been simple human ones, for example, the KELT designate who took ill, with a subsequent term's delay in filling the post; the perfect ELT teacher-supervisor designate in a provincial education office who was offered a scholarship to the University of Sierra Leone and

(who can blame him?) took it. Such problems are inevitable and predictable
— the difficulty of finding twelve motor-bike-riding, ELT or primary
qualified VSOs; the Sierra Leonean counterparts who get trained and, when
and if they can, move on within a few years to better things; the KELT who
decides two years is enough for his children's health/education or his own
health/career prospects; the VSO who has an unhappy love affair, or malaria
(or both!). The potential problems are unlimited and mind-boggling.

All we can do is try, through steady, solid work, to implement what seems
like a reasonably feasible plan, but be open to the need for change or adaptation of that plan whenever and wherever it might occur. And after all, even
if we only achieve half of what we set out to do, that half will count for more
than something in Sierra Leone, which, as a typically African aid-worthy
context, has seen more than its fair share of plans and projects, but precious
little in the way of achievements. We hope, indeed, that the planning of our
project has its achievements built in, but if time proves to us that this is not
the case, then our priority must be to achieve something of value in the
circumstances, not to follow a clearly mistaken or outdated project plan, no
matter how commendable its approach, how neat and symmetrical its form,
how attractive and persuasive its presentation.

MATERIALS DESIGN IN AFRICA WITH PARTICULAR REFERENCE TO THE FRANCOPHONE PRIMARY-SCHOOL PROJECT, CAMEROON

PAUL WILSON and IAN HARRISON

Cameroon

Introduction

The English for francophone primary-schools project (EFPS project), which started in 1975, aims to introduce English into the last three classes in all the primary schools in the five francophone provinces of Cameroon. In general, francophone class teachers will teach English to their own classes. There are approximately 6000 classes involved so that at least 6000 teachers have to be trained to provide complete coverage. Teacher wastage effectively raises this number to 10,000.

By July 1982, approximately 1700 student teachers will have passed through the one-year pre-service course, and the same number of teachers already working in the schools will have received at least one two-day in-service course. The textbook the teachers have been trained to use has been written as part of the project. The first two books have already been published and are being used in the schools. The third book is ready for printing and will be published this summer (1982).

1. Project background

A brief account of the background of the project will show the different strategies concerning teacher supply and learning materials that were tried during the first three years (1975–1978).

When the project first started it was envisaged that there would be an adequate supply of trained anglophone primary-school teachers coming from the training colleges in the two anglophone provinces who would be available for posting as English teachers in the primary schools in the five francophone provinces. Unfortunately this projected supply of anglophone teachers did not materialize; neither was it foreseen that the anglophone teachers who *were* trained and posted to the francophone zone would be concentrated in the schools in the five provincial capitals, schools elsewhere being more or less neglected.

The first attempt to meet the shortfall of teachers was a plan to train those students whose level of English was sufficiently high in each of the francophone training colleges. A pilot scheme was set up in one training college in 1977 and by 1979 forty-six francophones had been trained to teach English. During the fourth year of the project (1978–1979) it was realized that even if this pilot scheme had been adopted in all the francophone training colleges, approximately twenty-five years would have been needed before full coverage of the schools could hope to be achieved.

From 1979, therefore, the francophone training colleges have incorporated into their curriculum 10 hours of English a week (language improvement and methodology) for *all* their students. At the same time as this pre-service training has been given, short in-service ELT training courses have been run for those francophone teachers whose English is of a sufficiently high standard (at least equivalent to that of the poorer training college graduate).

During the first three years of the project a set of teaching notes was written and revised; these notes were intended at first for the anglophone teachers and then for the small numbers of francophone teachers coming from the training colleges. They were written in English and were therefore immediately unsuitable for the new, low-level type of francophone teacher to be recruited. Even if they had been translated into French they would have still been unsuitable since pedagogical advice and linguistic information were combined in such a way as to confuse even the average *anglophone* teacher. Moreover, the teacher was not shown how to break up the units into individual classroom lessons. The type of teacher recruited from October 1979 onwards needed much more detailed and structured assistance. The original teaching notes were therefore abandoned and new materials developed; these comprised three pupils' and teachers' books, the design of which was profoundly influenced by the teachers, the pupils and the situation they were intended for.

It may be wondered why over three years should have elapsed before it was realized that the wrong operating strategies had been adopted. One answer is that any project team, any individual even, must be constantly examining past and projected progress and changing strategies in the light of experience or because of changes in the client's administrative policy when it is clear that nothing, or very little that is effective, is being achieved.

A discussion of what went wrong in the early stages of this particular project, together with a set of suggestions for the successful planning, organization and implementation of future materials writing projects will, it is hoped, prove useful to current and future ELT work in other Third World countries.

Mountford (1981) has already expressed the view that all ELT materials writing operations should be designed 'projects' and that therefore they should be subject to a 'project approach'. He talks of:

making available for reference and scrutiny a clear specification of what a programme is all about: who does what, with whom, to what ends and why; with what resources; on what time scale; and how.

Unfortunately very little of this approach can be said to have been applied initially to the Cameroon EFPS project. The result was not only that individual experts seemed to be working in a vacuum in their own narrowly defined areas or that available or needed resources were rarely identified until it was too late, but also, as mentioned earlier, that the operating strategies adopted by, or for the team, turned out to be unsuccessful in realising the long-term aims of the project.

What was apparently lacking? There appeared to be:

> little or no initial project design or effective briefing of appointees; the three members of the team who arrived at post in 1975 were apparently left to their own devices to do what they could as best they could before the arrival of the materials writer and the project co-ordinator in 1976; neither did a time schedule seem to have been worked out;
>
> no period of time for consultations or observation by the team so that the initial project design could be 'deepened'; strategies consequently turned out to be the wrong ones;
>
> no rigorous trialling of the materials; this would quickly have revealed their inadequacies;
>
> no decision-making by the team or an advisory committee on the materials themselves; the design and content may well have been altered if this had been done;
>
> no apparent teaching of the materials by the team in the classrooms where the materials were to be used and where the trained teachers were to be working; this, we feel, is essential if the materials writer is not to lose touch with reality;
>
> no consultations with or visits by headquarters; this kind of support is essential in the early years at least;
>
> no close examination of the projected teacher-supply figures taking into account the reality of the situation; it is all too easy to state that the required number of teachers will or has been produced and that the project has therefore been successful, conveniently using statistics to conceal, for example, the teacher drop-out rate or the unequal distribution of trained teachers; the number of teachers trained does not necessarily equal the number of classrooms where English is in theory being taught.

2. Suggestions for project design

With the above assessment in mind we should like to develop further the ideas on the various essential phases in a project that were put forward by one of the groups at the 1981 Dunford House seminar on Evaluation and Testing.

Diagram 1 represents schematically the steps that ideally should be taken at all stages to ensure a final product which is wholly effective and acceptable in the educational system in which it is to be used and which can be produced with the maximum degree of efficiency and cost-effectiveness.

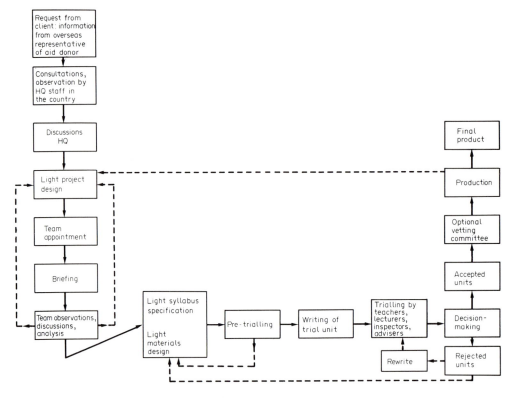

DIAGRAM 1

After observation and consultations in the host country by one or, preferably, more than one member of headquarters staff—with the client, with experts already working there and with representations of the aid-donor—and after further discussion at headquarters so that a wider, more composite view can be obtained, a 'light' or predictive project design can be formulated. This comprises first the resources that can realistically be provided by the client and those that must be provided by the donor, and, second, such items as aims and objectives, staffing, functions, counter-parting, teacher-supply, time-schedules, etc.

The process of 'deepening' the light design, i.e. certain strategies may be abandoned or modified and others adopted, will begin once the team members arrive at post; indeed it may well start before the team leaves for post—indeed we should like to see the briefing period extended to provide an opportunity for thought and discussion by the team on the initial project design, in consultation with headquarters staff. We should also like to see the content of the briefing itself made much more structured and relevant, using as a starting-point British Council, KELT or UNDP reports on previous or current projects with similar aims elsewhere in the world — this will probably occur anyway as the planning of projects becomes more structured.

The initial light project design may continue to be deepened more or less throughout the life of the project, factors and constraints that were not apparent at the planning stage emerging through the trialling, the team consultations or through the actual production of the materials. The problems encountered during the production of the first book of the Cameroon materials provide a good illustration of how even factors emerging during the production stage can deepen the initial design. The time-scale promised by the host-country publisher was hopelessly optimistic, as was their assessment of their capabilities and resources as regards design, setting-up, proof-reading and illustration of the book. Our design was there-fore modified so that the two subsequent books were published as a joint venture between a British publisher and the host-country printers.

The light syllabus specification drawn up after the team consultation period will be gradually deepened by the trialling which, together with the pre-trialling (a less rigorous trying-out of different language activities, games and exercises), will also deepen the light materials design formulated at the same time.

The decision whether to accept, modify or reject a particular unit in the light of the trialling will be taken by one or more of the following: the writers; the whole team; an advisory committee (Ministry officials, aid-donor represen-tation at home and in the host country, etc.).

It must be stressed that the above is an ideal model and that constraints such as time, money, human factors and other practical problems will tend to modify it in practice. Nevertheless, in the light of our experience with the EFPS project, we feel that these are the steps that should be followed as far as possible.

The role of constraints in materials design

The first task demanded of all materials writers, especially those producing a book for a specific context, is to make a leap of imagination and put themselves in the place of the teachers who will be using their book. They must assess the capabilities of the teachers and their pupils, the conditions they will be working under, the resources available to the teachers, and the various factors which militate against or work towards the success of what they will be asking their teachers to do. In order to clarify their thoughts they will produce a rationale in which they will not only set out all the relevant information in as orderly way as possible, but will also attempt to make certain predictions about the design and content of the finished book and about the development of any teacher-training programme which either exists or which will be set up to ensure that teachers can cope with the materials and the methodology involved.

Certain factors will present themselves from the start, but others will only emerge over a period of time. What will occur is a continuing tension between what the writers would like to do, especially by way of innovation, and what they are allowed to do by the constraints or by events occurring after the rationale has been written. Initially, the writers' preconceptions of what should occur in the classroom will lead them to minimize the strength of the constraints so that they will tend to propose in their rationale strategies which later they will either have to modify or discard.

We intend here to outline the main constraints apparent when we began to work on the books under discussion, to show how these constraints helped to shape the design and content of the books together with the methodology to be employed, and finally to describe the changes which took place in the light of the trialling of the material.

As mentioned earlier, the aim was to produce three books, each one constituting a year's work, for the final three years of the Cameroonian francophone primary school, that is, Cours Elémentaire 2, Cours Moyen 1 and *Cours Moyen 2*, of the Cameroonian francophone primary school. Both writers had several months' experience of what went on in the schools by virtue of their respective positions and, more important, by virtue of the fact that they had taught two classes on a regular basis in a Yaounde primary school. The principal factors which they had to take into account and which will be found in most other countries in Africa are outlined below:

Classrooms:
   dark, small and dusty;
   corrugated iron roofs which during rainstorms produce a lot of noise;
   usually no floor to ceiling dividing wall resulting in a high noise level
      spilling over from adjoining classrooms.

Classes:
   size on average sixty-five but often rising to eighty or ninety and oc-
      casionally to over a hundred;
   include the whole ability range; the best pupils can read, write and speak
      French well while the worst can hardly read and write at all although
      they can usually speak French;
   have an age range of as much as three years in the same class because of
      pupils having to double or treble a year if they fail the end of year
      examination.

Facilities in the schools:
   no electricity;

no staffroom;
no cupboards or other storage space;
often no chalk;
usually no stocks of paper or card;
blackboards often small and in a state of disrepair;
no reprographic facilities.

Teaching methods:
academic in content and approach;
French is taught on the whole by grammatical description methods;
authoritarian and teacher dominated;
the class is taught as a whole and group work is unknown;
great emphasis on copying and correctness;
much choral repetition;
frequent testing and much importance attached to written termly
    examinations;
harsh discipline.

Children:
the age range is anywhere from 9 to 12 in Cours Elémentaire 2 to 12 to
    16 in Cours Moyen 2; their behaviour is typical in that they behave
    with a teacher who can keep discipline, and misbehave with one who
    cannot;
their attention span is short and activities must be varied and well
    organized to sustain their interest;
they tend to become excited during certain activities in the English
    lesson when freed from the rigid discipline of other lessons; good,
    experienced teachers can control this; the brighter ones like learning
    English, but the attitude of the majority depends greatly on the skill
    of the teacher in maintaining the impetus of the lesson.

Time scale:
twenty-five effective teaching weeks in the school year after monthly,
    termly and annual examinations, public holidays, school holidays,
    preparation for parades, etc. have been taken into account;
a three-year course.

Difference in progress in English between classes and between schools:
at the moment headmasters effectively decide whether or not and how
    much English is done although an official decree is to be published
    requiring one English lesson of half an hour to be given once a day,
    five days a week;
female teachers are entitled to four months maternity leave;
teachers often arrive well after the start of the school year;
teachers often absent themselves to enquire about salary problems.

Teacher supply:

> as mentioned earlier, future teachers were to be francophones teaching English to their own classes and possibly to another one or two classes in the same school; they would have little or no time to prepare English lessons; they would comprise all the future graduates of the Ecoles Normales d'Instituteurs Adjoints (ENIA) and selected francophone teachers already in the schools who had volunteered to teach English;

> a few anglophone teachers would continue to be recruited but their numbers would be minimal — 300 out of the 10,000 we estimated were required for the implementation of the programme.

Standard of the teachers:

> all ENIA students have had four years of English in the secondary school; the quality of this instruction is, on the whole, suspect, with the result that most are false beginners;

> the test given to practising francophone teachers was designed to exclude anyone below the level of the poorer ENIA students;

> some anglophone teachers have been trained in ESL at the training colleges in the anglophone provinces while others have not been trained at all; they all receive one or two days' training in EFL once they start teaching in the francophone primary schools.

Teacher resources:

> we decided that all teachers had to be given a copy of Teachers' Books 1, 2 and 3 (which include all the material in the Pupils' books) by the Ministry of Education since if teachers had to buy their own books, few would do so and very little English would be taught.

Pre-service teacher training courses:

> the ENIA students follow a one-year course (in reality sixteen weeks' classroom teaching) with 10 hours a week devoted to English (language and methodology); ENIA teaching staff are mainly Cameroonian graduates of the University of Yaounde and of the Ecole Normale Superieure, most of whom have no training in EFL; they are constantly being posted so that there is little continuity.

In-service teacher training courses:

> the francophone teachers already in the schools will receive on average one two-day in-service course in their first year of teaching English; some may have another course in subsequent years, many will not;

> the selection of these teachers has been organized by the Provincial Inspectors (British Council recruited staff) who also design and administer the in-service courses;

> Cameroonian counterparts will, in theory, take over from them by the time they leave in July 1982.

All these factors were known while the design and content of the future textbooks were still being formulated. Their relative importance was also appreciated so that it could be fairly safely predicted which would become powerful constraints and which would be peripheral. For example, teachers who are false beginners constitute a more powerful constraint than a lack of electricity in the classroom. Nevertheless, all were included in the textbook rationale since predictions are never foolproof.

On the basis of our observations we chose a dialogue as the core of each lesson in Book 1 and immediately the constraints began to make themselves felt both on the material and on the methodology. Given the size of the classes and the need to allow each child to speak English as much as possible, it was decided that the children would repeat the dialogue after the teacher two or three times. So that the children would be given a chance to deduce the meaning of what they were saying, the teacher would then ask for the French equivalents. If they could not work out the meanings for themselves, the teacher would tell them. To introduce an element of role-play these steps would then be followed; the class would be divided in two, each half taking the part of one of the characters; they would then change roles; two individuals would stand up and act out the dialogue, thus allowing the brighter pupils to show their paces and introduce variations; finally each child would practise the dialogue with his or her neighbour.

Since the general level of the teachers was so low, both in their ability to use English and in their ability to handle dialogues even after training, it was felt to be essential to produce a formula such as the one outlined above. The minimal in-service courses together with the short duration of the pre-service courses, the latter being given by Cameroonian teachers who were themselves not EFL specialists, precluded anything more innovative in form and content. Other aspects of the dialogue and how they were to be handled were also related to the constraints:

    because of difficulties encountered by the teachers in managing dia-
        logues of three or more people, each dialogue had to be as far as
        possible between only two people;
    because of the concentration span of primary-school children the dia-
        logues were limited to four lines;
    because of the crowded classrooms and the time element, individuals
        had to stand and say the dialogue where they were, and not come to
        the front of the class and act it;
    choral repetition was already an accepted part of teaching in other
        lessons;
    the set pattern of exploiting the dialogue meant that it could be com-
        pleted in the time allotted to it (see later);
    the teacher controlled the whole process except for the pair work (this is
        dealt with later), and so felt secure in his traditional role of directing
        what went on in the classroom.

We felt that the same constraints which affected the dialogue would also influence the other parts of each lesson and that it would therefore be sensible to have a fixed lesson format throughout the first book. As anglophone teachers had had such difficulties with making separate lessons out of the previous materials, we assumed that francophones would have even greater problems and so decided that each lesson in the book would represent a lesson of half an hour in the classroom.

Each dialogue would need to be revised in the following lesson so a simple and short formula was devised for doing this. This revision was given 5 minutes at the beginning of each lesson while the dialogue for that lesson was expected to be covered in 10 minutes.

Since the children always grew restive after 20 minutes of oral work it was a natural step to devote the last 10 minutes of each lesson to written work of some kind and/or drawing. Other factors were also involved in this decision:

> those children without books would have some written English to take away at the end of the course, and would be equipped to revise for tests and examinations;
> written work would confer respectability on the subject and give it the same status as other subjects, especially French;
> it would provide a break for both the teacher and the children after what is, in an overcrowded classroom in the tropics, an exhausting 20 minutes.

The content of this part of the lesson would have to be simple enough for the less able to at least attempt it and yet demanding enough for the more able to have enough to do and to gain satisfaction from doing it. It would also have to be set out in such a way that the teachers could administer it easily.

We wanted to give the children an opportunity to use the language items they had learned in different contexts and situations and so devised oral exercises which could only last 5 minutes aimed at providing this practice which we placed after the dialogue. Again the same constraints which had operated before limited what could be done — the size of the classes, the low level of the teachers, the quality and amount of training the teachers would receive, the need to reassure the teacher that he was in full control of the activity, the time allowed for the exercise, etc. All these stipulated that the exercises be fairly similar throughout the book so that the teachers could be taught to handle them competently, hence the need for a formulaic procedure.

Obviously 125 lessons all most or less the same in content and form would soon fail to stimulate even the most disciplined class. Besides, the writers wanted to introduce activities traditionally associated with primary-school learning such as games, crosswords, puzzles, songs, rhymes and riddles. But yet again the familiar constraints came into play. Where these activities were introduced, they had to be simple enough for the teachers to be able to manipulate them. We had to take into account the fact that:

> group work is alien to the Cameroonian primary-school classroom;
> even materials such as paper and card are not available;
> everything the teachers are expected to do has to be taught in the pre-service and in-service courses;
> teachers do not read the teacher's notes if they are too voluminous;
> space is cramped with usually four children sharing a bench and desk designed for two, making movement difficult and limiting the types of activity which are practical.

With all these factors taken into consideration the first twenty-five lessons were written and sent off for trialling. The trialling instrument itself is described in the next section. It soon became clear that certain initial assumptions would have to be revised.

Because we had both had reasonable exposure to the conditions in the classrooms, including teaching the old materials to primary classes on a regular basis, and knew the standard of the teachers, we were able to write the materials with these specific conditions in mind. We could therefore work out how the dialogues, exercises and other activities would be presented and exploited as we wrote them, ensuring that we included nothing that we could not do ourselves in the same situation, and bearing in mind that even after training the teachers would in general perform at a much lower level of efficiency than ourselves. Nevertheless, when we began trialling we found that once we had distanced ourselves from the classroom and started writing the materials, we had made the usual errors of including too much material in each lesson and producing material which was too difficult for the children. Completed questionnaires revealed that teachers were not completing some lessons and were experiencing difficulty with some of the exercises. These lessons were rewritten and the trialling of subsequent lessons showed that these particular mistakes were not generally repeated.

A major constraint which was not apparent in the formal trialling classes where each pupil was provided with a roneoed copy of the lesson, came to light when the ENIA students went on teaching practice. Their pupils did not have copies of the lessons and it soon became clear that not only would the dialogues have to be copied on the blackboard, but also key words and drawings in the speaking exercises and the whole of the writing exercises. This obviously limited still further the amount of material which could be included in a lesson. It was reasonable to suppose that the same situation would arise in the future in classes where a significant proportion of the pupils would not, for various reasons, have the Pupils' Book — a correct supposition as it turned out. We now had to keep in mind that while a teacher would have the Teachers' Book, very few or none of his pupils might have the Pupils' Book; this necessitated an even sparser and simpler design than the one we had started with.

This gradual simplification of what was already a book designed for the lowest common denominator of teacher continued throughout the trialling period although we were able to show the better teachers on the in-service courses and the students on the pre-service courses how this basic design could be improved upon. Role-playing activities did not work because of the low level of teacher sophistication, class size and cramped conditions, but some teachers were able to change the language in some of the exercises so that the children could give personal answers or could pretend they were someone else. Pair work was at first included but then rejected because of the chaos which ensued. However, it did seem to work after a time with the better, experienced teachers and so was reinstated, poorer teachers being advised to omit it if they could not control the class—many did this anyway. Songs and games were included, but puzzles, riddles, problems and jokes (which we had said in the Rationale we would include) were not, partly because even the simplest were above the ability of the children to do them and the teachers to exploit them, and partly because there was not enough room for them. With only 125 lessons in the year we found that five or six songs and a limited number of games which were simple to administer, and which the children enjoyed were more than sufficient, especially as the games had to be repeated fairly frequently so that the children and teachers became accustomed to them and could exploit them to the full. It emerged quite strongly in the trialling that certain games were extremely popular and that the pupils would have been prepared to play them every lesson. Others did not appeal at all or were not acceptable and were dropped.

The trialling of the first book suggested that the design we had adopted was working, and was popular with both teachers and pupils. We decided to continue with the same format in the second book with minor variations and the inclusion of slightly more complex activities, all of which were covered in the training programme. Again it seemed to be successful and popular. However, certain activities such as creative writing, small comprehensions and simple problem-solving activities which we had hoped to introduce were excluded because of the usual constraints. A major constraint in this respect turned out to be the fact that the classes were mixed ability as well as being large. Mixed-ability teaching has only proved a success in British secondary schools when the staff have been trained in the special techniques which this type of teaching involves. It is the same in Africa. If one wants to include an activity in a textbook which requires a certain expertise in the teachers for it to be carried out successfully, the teachers have to be taught this expertise.

The short duration of both the pre-service and in-service courses did not allow us to go far beyond the basic pedagogical skills that were in effect innovative as far as the students and teachers were concerned. It was the difficulty of training teachers that led us to adopt the same format for the third book. All the constraints which operated for the first two books and which precluded adopting a new format in the second book still existed, but the major factor was time. There was no time to train the student teachers to cope with a new design or a different approach, and in addition all the teachers who had already graduated from the ENIAs and those who had already attended an in-service course would have had to attend another course to be trained in the new techniques. This would have been an impossible task as the third book was finished in January 1982 and the team was due to leave in July 1982.

This, of course, emphasizes the importance of another constraint mentioned earlier, that of counterparting. Because of various factors, which are mentioned in the sections on trialling and evaluation, it is doubtful whether those who take over will be able to continue the training programme in the same way. One effect of this is that the textbook needs as far as possible to be teacher-proof so that no matter how inadequately trained the teacher may be, the children will learn something, and the lesson will have a certain cohesion so long as the teacher follows what is set out in the book. Further-more, as most of the ENIA lecturers teaching the pre-service course have little EFL experience or knowledge, and as there is no guarantee that any personnel who are sent to Britain for training will return to their old posts, the syllabus for the pre-service training course has to be as sparse and prescriptive as the textbook. It has to concentrate on certain basic formulas, which are repeated frequently.

The inability of most francophone teachers to operate confidently in English was one of the reasons for our putting all the rubrics of the first two books in French. Since the rubrics tend to follow a pattern and since most of the activities will be known by the time the children reach the third book, we phased out the French and replaced it with English in the last book.

Similarly, testing is important in the primary-school system, and it was evident that the vast majority of the teachers would be incapable of devising tests. There was neither the time nor the qualified staff to justify including a testing component in the pre-service course let alone the in-service courses, so termly tests had to be written into the Teachers' Book.

There is not space enough in this article to discuss and justify the decisions we took with regard to other factors affecting the textbook, but a list of such factors should be of interest to those engaged in similar work elsewhere in Africa.

1. Size and format of the Pupils' Book.
2. Layout of the Teachers' Book and its relation to the Pupils' Book.
3. Place of illustrations in the Pupils' Book.
4. Use of colour in the Pupils' Book.
5. Use of British English or another form of English.
6. Contracted forms versus non-contracted forms.
7. Transmission of errors by the teachers.
8. Use of loan words.

9. Inclusion of grammatical paradigms.
10. Correctness versus fluency and the effect upon the material.
11. Use of handwriting or print in the dialogues.
12. Use of the first foreign language or the vernacular.
13. Provision of regular tests for the teachers to give to the pupils.
14. Use of electronic aids—cassettes, etc.
15. Use of visual aids—figurines, wall charts, etc.
16. Exploitation of local media.
17. Supply of materials for the reproduction of the trialling units—ink, paper, etc.
18. Reprographic equipment, its maintenance and possible repair (and availability of spare parts).
19. Availability and quality of back-up staff such as typists, artist, etc.— are they readily available or just a promise?
20. What happens if the host country fails to provide what it has promised.
21. Time schedules for writing, trialling and production of materials—are they realistic?
22. Who will be printing the final product? If it is a local printing firm, has it the resources to keep to the production schedule?
23. What happens if the production schedule is not kept to?
24. What effect will late publication have on the introduction of the book into the schools?
25. Liaison with the Ministry of Education to ensure that circulars are sent out regarding the stipulated number of lessons per week, etc.; a complete infrastructure of decrees should be set up to safeguard the future continuance of the project.
26. Liaison with responsible people in the different ministries as to what is acceptable and what might be offensive.
27. Counterpart system—does it work? If not, what steps can be taken to ensure the materials can be used if teacher quality falls still further.

3. Trialling

We considered it essential to devise a procedure by which the design of the materials could be evaluated through the process of teaching and learning so that any necessary amendments could be made before the final printing.

The following is a checklist of the information on the appropriacy and effectiveness of the materials that we wished to have; the same parameters should also, we feel, be used when assessing existing materials.

1. Relevance to the age of the pupils.
2. Relevance to both male and female pupils.
3. Relevance to the pupils' needs or wants.
4. Level of difficulty—was a unit or a particular component of a unit too easy or too difficult?

5. Balance of activities — was there too much or too little of a particular component?
6. Amount of material — was a unit or unit component too long or too short for the time allowed?
7. Teacher attitudes — if teachers enjoyed or disliked a particular activity or a particular unit or the materials generally, we wanted to know the reasons.
8. Pupil attitudes — we wanted to know which activities were enjoyed or disliked by the pupils (and why).
9. Acceptability in terms of the local culture and political situation.
10. Appropriacy of teaching techniques — we wanted to know whether the methodology adopted was feasible with the target classes and whether it was suited to the physical environment.
11. Did the teachers find difficulty in handling any of the innovatory techniques? Could the teachers be trained to handle them?
12. Were the illustrations clear and useful?
13. Were the materials effective in terms of pupil learning?
14. Were the teaching notes (a) used, (b) clear, (c) effective?

One useful and unforeseen 'spin-off' of the trialling operation turned out to be its public relations and advertising role. We found that not only can trialling serve as a convenient vehicle for publicizing at all levels the aims and strategies of the project but also that it can provide an opportunity for large numbers of key local officials, who otherwise would not be involved, to become an integral part of the operation. Although the amount of information obtained from these officials is not necessarily significant, the amount of goodwill engendered is, we feel, well worth any effort made.

The information we required was obtained using two types of evaluation procedure — the pre-trialling, which was informal, and the trialling, which was intended to be more rigorous and formal.

The pre-trialling was done by the two writers in primary schools and in a training college before and during the writing of the trial materials; it concerned small, isolated items rather than the teaching of a whole section although a whole lesson was often taught. Whether not to include a particular game or activity was ascertained by this method, as was information on the amount of material which could be included in a particular lesson. If we ourselves could not finish a lesson within the specified time or teach a particular activity successfully then we could not expect our teachers to be able to do so. If the student teachers could not be taught to handle a particular aspect of the materials then the design of the materials had to be changed. In the absence of an advisory committee the pre-trialling period also enabled us to avoid any glaring errors in terms of political or cultural acceptability.

The formal trialling instrument had to be broad-based in order to take into account conditions prevailing throughout all five francophone provinces. In addition, in order to obtain as much information as possible, particularly about the minimally trained francophone teacher, the instrument had to include all the categories of teacher who would eventually be using the book. In each province, therefore, trialling took place in six classes (a total of thirty) taught as far as possible by the following types of English teacher:

1. An anglophone teacher who was trained[1] and/or experienced and/or good, to whom the KELT Provincial Inspector gave help and guidance in the use of the materials.[2]
2. An anglophone teacher who was untrained and/or inexperienced and/or mediocre, to whom the Inspector gave help and guidance.
3. An anglophone teacher who was untrained and/or inexperienced and/or mediocre, to whom the Inspector gave no help or guidance.
4. A francophone teacher who was trained and to whom the Inspector gave help and guidance.
5. A francophone teacher who was untrained and to whom help and guidance was given.
6. A francophone teacher who was untrained and to whom no help or guidance was given.

Initially at least, given the small number of francophone teachers at the beginning of the trialling, it was impossible to specify 'good' or 'mediocre' with the categories of francophone teacher in the trialling instrument — each Inspector had to use what personnel he could find in his area.

The trialling schools in each province were chosen so as to provide easy coverage of both rural and urban schools. Regular contact with all categories of trialling teacher was considered essential and it was important, therefore, to select convenient schools; fairly typical rural schools could anyway be found near all the urban centres.

Information on the trial materials was obtained in three ways:

a questionnaire;
discussions with the trialling teachers;
observations of these teachers in their classrooms.

We had already rejected the idea of a series of criterion-referenced tests to be given at intervals during the trialling on the grounds that this procedure would be impracticable, time-consuming and not very fruitful.

We felt that if the questionnaire were to be too long or too difficult to complete, teachers would not fill it in. Too complex a questionnaire might very well have antagonized some teachers, who were, after all, being asked to take on extra work. The questions were therefore couched in simple language and arranged in a format that was simple to follow and in which it was easy to insert (see Appendix 1). Since half the trialling teachers were francophone and since we wanted to be sure of their comprehension of the questions asked, a French version of the questionnaire was produced.

Following the collection of the questionnaires from the trialling teachers after each completed section of five classroom lessons, there was an informal talk, the purpose of which was to provide an opportunity for expressing views in an informal and relaxed way. Regular meetings of the trialling teachers in a particular area were also held so that views and ideas on the improvement of the materials could be put forward and discussed; these meetings also had the added public relations value of making the teachers feel part of the team. During the meetings the writers or the Provincial Inspectors were able to probe a little more deeply than could be done by a written questionnaire and thus find out what the teachers really thought rather than what they thought we wanted to hear.

The final method of obtaining feedback from the trialling teachers was by observation of their lessons; this provided immediate and first-hand information on the success or failure of particular activities or lessons. Moreover, from the observation of the trialling teachers' weaknesses the team was also able to obtain ideas for inclusion in the training courses.

One further method of obtaining information, particularly on the teachability of certain items, concerned the training-college student teachers. If, on the whole, these young and inexperienced teachers could be taught to successfully handle what was for them innovative techniques or activities that demanded certain classroom management skills, then these could be included in the revised version of the materials. This seems to us to be an important aspect of the trialling operation and one that is often neglected. After all, the decision facing the writers when dealing with activities or techniques that seem to be unsatisfactory in the light of the trialling, is whether to make a change in the design of the materials or whether to make an addition to the teacher-training course. If experience in the training colleges has shown that the teachers are capable of being trained to handle certain items but not others, then this is exactly the kind of information that the writers must have.

What problems were encountered during the trialling? The main practical problems arose from the unrealistic schedule forced upon us through the necessity to write, trial, revise and produce the three books in a little over three years. Although we made the trialling organization as simple and as streamlined as possible to take account of the practical difficulties of the Cameroon situation, two factors acted against a total trialling of the materials. First, the fact that the deadline for the completion of the manuscript had to be brought forward to the 31st January for it to be printed in the summer of the same year when it was realized that the capabilities of the local publisher were not going to be all that had been promised. The second reason for having to curtail the trialling was the length of time it took for the trial materials to reach the schools in the provinces and for the comments to come back to the writers. In practice, therefore, the first fifty lessons (out of 125) were extensively trialled in the first year (when the information obtained is the most valuable) while in the second and third years this was reduced to the first twenty-five. This was inevitable given the time schedule we were told to work to—three books in three years.

4. Evaluation

A proper evaluation of the materials is, we feel, better carried out by a different team who can distance themselves more easily. The evaluation of pupil performance can, in any case, only be most effectively done when pupils who have followed all three years of the course start emerging from the schools. This will not occur in this project until July 1983. Individual books of the course could be evaluated before this but since the three books are closely connected and have a cyclical structure, the results obtained would be more valid if all the books were included in the evaluation. As mentioned earlier, the parameters listed with reference to the trialling should provide much evaluative information although a criterion-referenced test, given in a broad sample of classrooms, is the best method of evaluating the materials in terms of pupil performance.

Clearly it would be preferable if the materials could be evaluated in this way, but we are forced to ask ourselves whether it is realistic to expect it to happen. Who will devise, organize and administer the tests? Our counterparts, those few at least who have come back to the project, may well have the necessary training but will not have the necessary resources (transport, paper, stencils, duplicator, ink, etc.) to carry it out. Who will fund an operation of this kind? If it is deemed necessary to evaluate the materials, any accompanying teacher-training programme, indeed the project as a whole, then provision should be made for this at the project planning stage and in the project budget.

Notes

1. 'Trained' means that the teacher had received either pre-service or in-service training in EFL/ESL.
2. The question of 'help and guidance' was left up to the individual Provincial Inspector, but it was indicated that any future counterparts would not necessarily have the time, resources or even the inclination to run in-service courses or to make regular advisory visits, and that this factor should be borne in mind. As far as possible the aim was to duplicate the conditions that would prevail upon the departure of the team.

References

HARRISON, I. D. and WILSON, P., *The English for francophone primary schools project; texbook rationale.* June 1979.
MOUNTFORD, A., Design, evaluation and testing in English language projects. Paper presented at the 1981 Dunford House Seminar on Evaluation and Testing.
HIGGINS, J. and MOLLER, A. (Eds.) *Report on the 1981 Dunford House Seminar on Evaluation and Testing.*

APPENDIX I *QUESTIONNAIRE*

Please complete this questionnaire—write your answers in the spaces provided, using another sheet of paper if necessary.

Pupils' Book	a	b	c	d	e
Did the children enjoy the work in the lesson? If not, why not?					
Was there too much material in the lesson? If you didn't finish, where did you get to?					
Was there too little material in the lesson? If so, how many minutes before the end of the lesson did you finish?					
Were all the activities successful? If not, which one was unsuccessful and why?					
Did you have any difficulty teaching any part of the lesson? What was the difficulty?					

Teachers' Book	a	b	c	d	e
Were the lesson notes clear? Quote any lines you did not understand.					
Were the lesson notes helpful? Quote any lines which were not.					

APPENDIX II

8d   eight d

Sally forgets her sweets, and Amina forgets her purse.

Sally oublie ses bonbons, et Amina oublie son porte-monnaie.

Dialogue

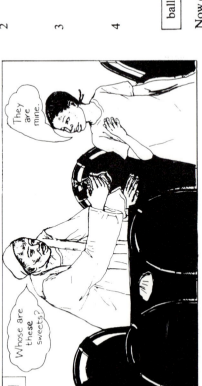

Speaking exercise

Le maître vous demande à qui appartiennent ces choses. Répondez-lui.

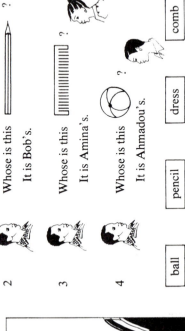

1   Whose is this
    It is Sally's.

2   Whose is this
    It is Bob's.

3   Whose is this
    It is Amina's.

4   Whose is this
    It is Ahmadou's.

Now do the same with your neighbour.

ball   pencil   dress   comb

Writing exercise

Copiez ces questions et réponses en y mettant les mots qui manquent

1   Whose is this dress?
    It is Sally's.

2   Whose is this _____?
    It is Ahmadou's.

3   Whose is this _____?
    It is Amina's.

THE ENGLISH LANGUAGE TEXTBOOK PROJECT— SOMALIA

DAVID CLARKE, HARRY HAWKES, NORMAN PRITCHARD and
BRIAN SMITH

Mogadishu, Somalia

Introduction

The following collection of papers is an attempt to give an account of the working of a textbook project in Somalia.

The project is financed by the ODA and administered by the British Council under the KELT scheme. Individual members of the team are responsible for the separate sections of the paper. It is hoped that the paper will be of interest to those working on or designing similar projects. One clear lesson that emerges from our experience is the need for flexibility — in the overall project strategy, in the writing and implementation and in the roles of the individual team members.

DESIGNING THE COURSE   BRIAN SMITH

The Republic of Somalia was formed by an amalgamation of the former British Somaliland Protectorate and the Italian Colony of Somalia. The amalgamation posed formidable problems of integration — legal, administrative and linguistic. English had been the major language of administration and education in the British-controlled North, and Italian in the South. Somali, the national language, spoken by virtually the whole population, still had no agreed script. A substantial number of Somalis, moreover, had been educated in Arabic and knew none of the European languages. After Independence there followed a period when administration was carried out in three languages: English, Italian and Arabic, while secondary education was increasingly conducted in English. Tertiary education was divided into two sections: the College of Education, which used English as the medium, and the remaining faculties which used Italian. The Revolution of 1969 brought into power a military-led government committed to Scientific Socialism, which in October 1972 took the decision, in the face of conservative opposition, to adopt the Roman script for Somali and to adopt the Somali language as the language both of administration and education, except at the tertiary level and in vocational and technical education. The situation in tertiary education remained as before, while English continued as the language of technical and vocational education.

The change obviously necessitated a radical rethinking of the English curriculum and the development or adoption of teaching materials suited to the new position of the English language in education. Various attempts were made but none was brought to a successful conclusion. In general, if materials were available at all they were more appropriate to an English-medium situation than to one in which English was merely a subject among others.

The present textbook project was set up as a result of a request by the Somali Ministry of Education to the British Council for assistance in the development of materials suited to the Somali environment. Originally the proposal was that these materials should be designed for beginning English in the fifth year of education, but for practical reasons it has been decided to postpone the start to the ninth year, i.e. the secondary level, adapting later if necessary to an earlier start. At the same time it was decided to produce a sample scientific English course and reader to prepare students in vocational and technical education for instruction through the medium of English. This course was completed and distributed before work began on the general English course.

The textbook project in Somalia has both a unique challenge and a unique opportunity. There is no competition from commercially published materials, and given the chronic shortage of foreign exchange, it is unlikely that any serious competition will be encountered. Thus the book is assured of universal adoption. At the same time, since it will be the only textbook available, it is vital that it be appropriate, pedagogically sound and culturally acceptable.

Design of the course began with a brief, impressionistic survey of the use of English in Somalia and a needs analysis. It is of course difficult, if not impossible, to predict precisely the uses to which any given secondary-school student will put his knowledge of English, but it is possible on the basis of the role of English in the community to make useful generalizations which will be reasonably valid for the majority. Besides these factors, account had to be taken of the means available for implementing a programme of language teaching. These are severely limited — overcrowded and poorly equipped classrooms; inadequately prepared teachers; poor blackboard surfaces and poor-quality chalk, and a virtually bookless environment.

The following general specifications were drawn up:

1. The course should be rooted in the Somali environment and reflect the experience and interests of Somali pupils.
2. The main principle of organization would be a grammatico-structural progression, but both presentation and practice would take account of the recent emphasis on language as communication.

3. The materials should be broken down into clear sections, each section corresponding to a unit of teaching time.

4. There should be frequent review sections and the materials should incorporate such study aids as a grammar summary, bilingual word lists and glossary.

5. The materials should be densely illustrated with pictures and diagrams of a functional, pedagogic nature serving both to clarify meaning and to facilitate communicative practice.

6. While a teachers' book would be prepared, the inherent methodology should be apparent from the students' book alone, which would contain both clear statements of what was to be learnt in each unit and an indication of the procedures to be followed by teacher and student.

7. The main aim of the course would be to prepare students to use English as a study language, emphasizing receptive skills, particularly reading. Hence vocabulary would not be too severely restricted, and the pacing of the course would be faster than might be the case in a course aiming at a high degree of productive ability.

8. Topics related to students' studies would be introduced as the course progressed.

9. While, for interest, material concerned with Britain might be introduced, it was no part of the intention of the course to provide an introduction to the culture of the English-speaking world.

When these broad specifications had been drawn up, the syllabus content for the first two volumes was specified in terms of a number of sequences, each expressed in notional/functional terms with linguistic exponents and suggested situations and topics. These varied considerably in detail because of the difficulty experienced in setting down precise specifications of all the linguistic content in a coherent set of sequences. The dynamic creative process was found in practice to impose many changes on the originally conceived sequences, both in the exponents and in the grouping and sequencing of categories.

The process of writing has itself undergone certain changes since the inception of the project. This is partly as a result of changes in the constitution of the team which originally consisted of a team leader, responsible for overall design and monitoring; a writer, responsible for drafting the teaching materials; a teacher trainer, based at the College of Education and responsible primarily for pre-service training of teachers of English, who also assumed responsibility for preparing teachers' books; a variable number of Somali counterparts who could be consulted on the cultural content and who prepared Somali versions of the glossary and rubrics. Fortunately the wife of the textbook writer is a talented artist and was willing to accept the post of layout artist/illustrator. (A feature of the materials is the close integration of the text and the illustrations made possible by the close collaboration of the writer and the illustrator.)

In the initial stages of writing — indeed for most of the first book — the text-book writer worked largely alone, writing the teaching units which were then submitted for comment to the other team members. With the advent of an additional team member whose primary responsibility is to monitor the teaching of the materials in the schools, it has been possible to introduce a greater element of team work in the original drafting of the materials. While the writer remains responsible for the final form taken by the material, other team members contribute in various ways through discussion of appropriate presentation and practice situations and procedures as well as by drafting materials which may either be incorporated unchanged or modified and adapted by the textbook writer. The final drafts are then examined by the team, discussed, amended and passed to the layout artist/illustrator for the preparation of photo-ready pages, the chosen method of reproduction being by offset litho. This method has the advantage of ensuring complete control of the page design, and choice of type and — even more important — it obviates the need for time-consuming proof-reading.

DESIGN CONSTRAINTS AND
TEXTBOOK ILLUSTRATIONS   NORMAN A. PRITCHARD

1. The constraints of printing economics

The writer of textbooks for national school systems in the developing world
operates normally within two categories of constraints. The first category is
that of the curriculum, a field in which the typical KELT officer will have a
great deal of general experience and specific training, ranging as it does from
the requirements of national politics down to such specifics as how many
students there may be in the average classroom. The second category —
overlapping rather separate from the first — has mainly to do with economics:
the economics of the printer/publisher, and this is an area in which many of
us have to confess to having little experience and almost no training
whatsoever. And yet these constraints may have a profound effect upon our
product — an effect almost as important as the major curricular decisions.
They will affect such areas as paper quality, page size, cover quality,
monochrome/colour, type of illustration (e.g. photograph or line-drawing),
amount of illustration, and most importantly perhaps, general format. This
last consideration covers such questions as the density of page-filling and
varieties of type face to be used, and also such major decisions as whether the
product shall be give-away (in which case the student can write in all his own
answers) or reuseable (in which case the student cannot). Some or all of these
areas of choice may be closed to the writer, or will at best be shared with him,
the final decision being made by an editor or even a printing manager for
financial rather than pedagogical reasons.

The Somalia textbook is not unusual in suffering some total constraints.
There is only one paper quality: a rather poor one, greyish in colour, and
allowing neither gloss nor white contrast. It has a high wood content, and
will yellow in sunlight. This imposes a second constraint: line drawings rather
than photographs, since the paper does not allow good photographic
reproduction. A third constraint is that for Book 1 at least we are obliged to
use monochrome for reasons of cost, though one extra colour may be
available for Book 2 onwards. Mitigating these constraints is the excellence
of the German technical team and their Somali colleagues who operate the
Printing Agency.

In other areas however, we are fortunate in having total choice. As regards
page size, we have been allowed to make a purely pedagogical decision in
choosing A4, a page size that gives us the optimum teaching page consistent
with such practical considerations as ease of carrying. It is a relatively large
format, but in the absence at that time of reducing techniques and
photocompositing, it allowed a reasonable size of illustration and catered for
the size of IBM golfball type faces. Even more important is the question of
page design: we design the entire page and it is photographed in the final
form that we give to it. No changes beyond those of proof reading are made

by any editing process, and this gives us a far more generous use of space to give pleasing balance to a page than is normally the case. No exercises have to be squeezed into inappropriate corners, and there is no restriction save that of common sense on the number of pages in each book, although we do try to keep within multiples of sixteen – the number of pages in a 'forme'.

Similarly there is no restriction in the amount of illustration used. A typical fifteen-page stretch of Book 2, for example, gives the following area distribution:

Print	*Picture*	*Space*
43 per cent	30 per cent	27 per cent

By space here we mean all that area on a page not inside the frame of a block of print or a block of illustration. Such a generous use (or waste, a publisher might say) of space and illustration is quite rare and gives the series a character and style which is probably unique in such a project. The only rules of economy that we operate under are personal quirks: we like to fill every page, and we don't like to split up exercises. Instead we use 'filler' jokes, aphorisms, cartoons, puzzles, etc.

2. The importance of illustration

In the light of this total freedom of design, it can be seen that the absence of a photographic reproduction facility and even the necessity of monochrome are not in themselves such debilitating restrictions as they might be, providing that one major requirement is met: that the personnel of a textbook project should include a professional illustrator. This is an area of expertise frequently overlooked in the design of a project. It is assumed that such things will be taken care of by the printer/publisher, or that a talent will emerge locally, to be paid for either by the host government, or out of project funds at rates similar to those of a typist. We take the personal view that illustration is so central to the *writing* as well as to *printing* of a textbook, that a much more closely planned collaboration is required between writer and artist than is normally the case. The Somalia project has such collaboration, but is it by coincidence rather than project design.

Where economics allow photographs, then naturally the same comments are true concerning collaboration between photographer and writer – or even photographer and artist and writer. In Somalia we long debated the inclusion of photographs despite the poor quality of reproduction. Good photographic illustration can certainly complement and even replace hand drawings; the total reality afforded by the camera adds glamour and 'magic', particularly to the indigenously produced textbook. It is of obvious interest-motivating power for the African student to see his country and his culture as the backdrop to the English lesson, and the photograph can provide a wealth of background detail that a hand-drawn illustration can scarcely hope to illustrate. The North Yemen textbook uses photographs very successfully to make up for the lack of a professional artist, and it is undoubtedly true that while a textbook writer with no artistic talent is unlikely to learn to draw, he or she can expect to learn how to use a camera with some competence.

However, photographs have a major drawback if they are required for specific as opposed to general illustration work, and that is the amount of time it may take to set up and rehearse a scene or a sequence. Book 1 in a series typically uses a family or some other group to carry the story line, and the members of that group illustrate the teaching points. To get such a group organized for photographic sessions is difficult enough; to get amateurs to hold poses for still pictures without looking wooden and self-conscious is even more so. Unless studio facilities are available, the photograph is not always as clear as was intended, especially when reproduced by the printing process, and it may be days — or weeks — before defects in the pictures are discovered if the processing is not done immediately. Another problem where photographs are being taken as the book progresses is that caused by the absence of one of the actors, which may necessitate writing out a character ('Isn't Ahmed lucky, he has a scholarship to England!'). It is true that careful prior planning might avoid such a situation; photographic sessions could be organized only when the entire book was written. However, this almost certainly rules out trialling of the illustrations as well as the text, and furthermore it implies a precision of organization uncharacteristic of the textbook writing process as we know it, and perhaps even undesirable since overmethodical planning can stifle the creative aspect of the work.

3.   Functions of illustration-types in the Somalia textbooks

None of the above drawbacks occur with hand-drawn illustrations, where the only limitations will be the technical ones of reproduction (how far shading or wash techniques can be used, for example) and the personal style of the illustrator. Assuming that the illustrator is a full-time team member, the writer has almost total flexibility at his disposal: a drawing can be as large or as small, as simple or as complex, as focused or as general, as realistic or as cartoon-like as is desired. More than this, because of the intervention of the artist the pictures may well have aesthetic qualities that will transcend the function of the textbook as an ELT device and transform it into a vehicle for the education of the student in a far more general sense: in terms of appreciation of beauty; of form and balance; of dignity and respect. These may sound grandiose aims, but it must be remembered that in Somalia a student's contact with his textbooks may be his *only* contact with books. In this situation of a book-hunger almost as intense as that for food, every subject-author is obliged to remember that he or she is an educator first and an English or history or science teacher next.

In general we have adopted simple line drawings because of their reproduce-ability. We decided on realism rather than impressionism because of the lack of visual education in the culture — there are no cartoon strips, for example, and extreme cartoon styles proved to be incomprehensible. We rejected shading Somalis darker than Europeans since black no more represents the one than does white the other, and we find that the graceful Somali physique is easily recognizable from its lines alone. In the light of these general considerations we find ourselves using illustrations in the following ways:

1. For the introduction of characters and continuity of identity. Books 1 and 2 share the same characters, and much use has been made of the plain paper copier to ensure exact copies. At the beginning of Book 1 great care was taken to give the characters as recognizable a face as possible, so that later a more simple line drawing would suffice.
2. For the introduction of role: the father as a driver, the daughter as a nurse, the son as an electrician, etc.
3. For the introduction of setting: the thorn tree, the camel, the ubiquitous goat, recognizable city and village backgrounds, all give the 'feel' of Somalia to the text and therefore add to its attraction. No previous textbook has been able to do this because of the scarcity of local artists.
4. For the introduction of lesson theme, both general and specific.
5. As the stimulus to individual exercises.
6. As a cartoon-setting for dramatic interest: this is a relatively far-reaching innovation, since as was previously mentioned there are no cartoons in Somali printing to date, and very few foreign comics or newspapers or magazines are available to the average Somali.
7. As a wallchart: normally a blown-up version of an illustration in the book.

Each of the first six of the above illustration types is exemplified in the following samples. We hope it can be seen from them how integral are illustrations to the textbook — and therefore the teaching/learning process as we see it in Somalia.

1. *INTRODUCTION OF CHARACTERS*

2. *THE ROLE OF THE CHARACTERS.*

3. INTRODUCTION OF SETTING

They listened and started to fight for their freedom.

Ali Hussein was a very productive poet. During the period 1942 - 1950 he produced more than 200 patriotic poems.

4. INTRODUCTION OF THEME

BIGGEST AND SMALLEST

BIGGEST

BIGGER

BIG

5. INDIVIDUAL EXERCISE STIMULUS

5.2.2.   Do you remember Ahmed Bashir's accident ?   He is telling John Martin about it.

LESSON 6.4.

Going ... Going ... Gone

6.4.1.

THE TEACHER-TRAINING COMPONENT   HARRY HAWKES

Introduction

A fundamental requirement for the success of any new school textbook is the teachers to put the book effectively into use. We are fortunate to find that Somalia has a history of close contact with the English language and that there are teachers with a reasonable command of the language already in the schools.

But language teaching in Somalia has been in the doldrums for some time and teachers, lacking a standard textbook, have been forced to concoct a hotch-potch of language materials taught from the blackboard and usually accompanied by grammatical (mis)information. The KELT textbook, *English for Somalia (EFS)*, introduces a completely new approach to language teaching for these teachers and they will have to be weaned from their blackboard and chalk, and a grammatical terminology way above the heads of pupils, to a free technique of teaching which will use to advantage the illustrations and communicative exercises of *EFS*

1. In-service training

We had hoped to achieve this weaning by means of in-service courses held in the different regions of Somalia prior to the introduction of EFS into the secondary schools. But we found that such courses are not part of teachers' lives in Somalia; and the organization of the courses ran into administrative problems. It has been decided, therefore, to concentrate efforts on a back-up service to teachers in schools. This will involve visits to schools, usually in the company of the project Implementation Officer. Luckily, most of the secondary schools in Somalia are clustered round the two main cities, Mogadishu and Hargeisa. Even so, regular visits to schools will put a considerable strain on project manpower and resources.

The main efforts during the visits will be:

(a) to show teachers what *can* be done in the classroom with the new textbook, by means of demonstration lessons;
(b) to soothe them over any doubts about their own ability to use the book in the same way as demonstrated;
(c) to take round supplies of professional 'goodies' to encourage them in their efforts—dictionaries, vocabulary books, wallcharts, etc.

A lot of this work will be on a 'public relations' basis, therefore. Though it should be said that the Somali teachers we have encountered so far are an enthusiastic lot and will not need much persuasion.

It is hoped also to extend in-service help to teachers through a weekly column on ELT in the local English-language newspaper. This possibility is still under discussion with the Somali authorities.

Teachers have indicated, too, that they would welcome a specialist journal dealing with ELT. The chance of this is slim, due to the tight control on such publications in Somalia, but the suggestion is a mark of the enthusiasm of teachers.

2. Pre-service training

The National University of Somalia, in its College of Education, operates an ELT speciality course. For KELT, this is a *point d'appui* which not all textbook projects have − e.g. KELT Yemen lacks this.

However, there are drawbacks:

(a) The College of Education was established at a time when entrant students were using English as the medium of instruction in secondary schools; the College English curriculum was geared (and remains geared) to the standards of near-native performance in the language, and it concentrates heavily on literature; Somali secondary schools, meanwhile, have abandoned English as the medium of instruction and do not even teach the language effectively as a foreign tongue.

(b) College authorities are much concerned with the academic image of the institution, and are reluctant to revise the English language curriculum to meet the more practical language needs of today's entrants.

(c) The normal three-year college course, leading to a B.A. degree, has been concertinaed into two years due to the shortage of teachers in an expanding education system; this leads to 'semesters' of about ten weeks' duration and to the axing of the period of teaching practice; students graduate as teachers without ever having had the chance to stand in front of a class.

3. KELT teacher-training at the college

ELT methodology courses at the College of Education are hampered by the lack of a period of teaching practice; even peer teaching sessions are limited by the shortness of time in the ten-week semesters. However, methodology courses have been taught under the KELT project at the college since 1980 even while the KELT textbooks have been in preparation.

Students take a two-semester course in ELT methodology which up to now has been organized as follows:

Semester 1 − practical ELT techniques:
        'approaches' to ELT (structural, functional, communicative, etc.),
        'method' in ELT (selection, grading, sequencing),

teaching techniques for the four skills (peer teaching),
lesson plans,
testing,
audio-visual aids.
Semester 2 — linguistic theory related to ELT techniques:
language acquisition,
'grammars'
psycholinguistics,
sociolinguistics,
curriculum, syllabus, textbook.

Other college course in the ELT speciality cover phonology, grammar and history of the language.

Two groups of students have already gone through this methodology course, the second group with the benefit of referring to mimeographed trial copies of EFS. These students were the last to emerge from secondary schools having used English as the medium of instruction; with them, time could be saved for peer teaching by using a certain amount of straightforward lecturing. Their English was good enough, too, to allow a fair amount of class discussion on techniques and theories.

From 1982, new entrants to the college will be deficient in English, and it is not clear how many (if any) will be suitable candidates for the ELT speciality. Methodology courses will have to be organized on a very flexible basis and will have to concentrate on grassroots language skills as well as the classroom techniques needed by a teacher. The courses in 1982 will probably cover:

(a) thorough grounding in the vocabulary and patterns of *EFS*, Books 1 and 2, to ensure that potential teachers are competent at least in this level of language (luckily, Somalis have an impressive aptitude for languages, though this is often limited to the oral skills — reading and writing are, in general, badly done and betray the lack of solid practice in the written form of their own language);
(b) study of how language structures are developed in *EFS* (selection, grading, sequencing) and how they are used ('communication', 'function');
(c) study and practice of the techniques needed for teaching *EFS*, Books 1 and 2 — presenting, drilling, practising, revising, testing; teacher's notes are already available for Book 1 and give detailed help with lesson steps for the first Units, in an attempt to make the book 'teacherproof'. Later units are treated more briefly in the notes, and aim to help the teacher himself understand the vocabulary and structures that he is using. The notes will be continued for later books.

No extravagant sallies will be made into the super-duper ELT techniques of

European classrooms. Somali schools are desperately ill-equipped with teaching aids and sometimes even the teacher's presence cannot be relied upon. (The very specific rubric of *EFS* is again an attempt to make the book 'teacherproof' and as near to a self-study text as possible.) The English learned will be firmly based on what is printed on the pages of the textbook, from the point of view of both the language content and the exercises to practise it. For this reason, very little in the way of extension exercises have been included in the teacher's notes; it is felt that teachers will be doing very well to cope with what the textbook demands of them, without trying their professionalism (at the moment) with more imaginative exercises.

It is hoped to continue, with 1982 students, an experiment begun with present students of the College of Education. As the final part of their work for their degree, students have to research and write a thesis-type 'senior paper'. Previously, most of these senior papers have been on literary topics ranging from 'Beowulf' to the African novel. The ELT specialists, in 1981, undertook topics connected with the KELT textbooks and provided valuable feedback (prior to the introduction of the books into the schools) on such aspects as:

— potential problems in EFS for the Somali teacher and pupil;
— the rationale behind writing a special ELT textbook for Somalia;
— economics of textbook production in Somalia.

Students also worked on the lexis of Book 1 and built up the initial stages of a simple bilingual dictionary and a vocabulary book—two teaching aids badly missed in Somalia. It is hoped to produce a vocabulary book for each year of the KELT course; and to include finally in the dictionary all the 6000 or so words of the complete textbook course.

Students leaving the College of Education and going into the field will receive the same back-up visits as their colleagues already in service. Because of their close contact with the trialling copies of *EFS*, Book 1, college students may well become the focal point of the English work in their schools.

4. Two problems

1. One problem still to solve is the orienting of teachers for the more advanced teaching required by the later books in the textbook series, when they will be dealing with the use of English in study skills; something which very few of them have any experience of. We hope by that time to have found an answer to the problem of organizing in-service courses.

2. The actual supply of trained graduates to the secondary schools is outside the control of the project, and unfortunately there is a tendency for the most promising students to be creamed off for other jobs—in the Ministry of Information, in cultural work, etc. As in many Third World countries,

training in a foreign language is often seen as a qualification for some post other than the one the man was trained for. There is already a severe shortage of English teachers in the secondary schools. The success of any overseas textbook project will ultimately depend on the commitment of the host government to putting the right people into the classrooms.

EVALUATION OF *ENGLISH FOR SOMALIA*   David J. Clarke

Evaluation of the *English for Somalia* (henceforth EFS) programme is essential to the success of the project since the package of textbooks, teacher's notes and readers involves quite a considerable shift of approach for English language teaching and learning in Somali secondary education. It is vital that the pedagogic innovations to be introduced in *EFS* are successfully implanted especially in view of its projected lifetime of 10-15 years; the course therefore must be acceptable to administrators, practitioners and consumers as well as being fully practicable in Somali schools. Systematic and ongoing evaluation can contribute in no small measure to the effectiveness of the new programme.

Evaluation, then, is considered by the team to be a core activity in all stages of the project. Evaluated data provides or has provided the basis for judgements to be made on:

(a) the nature of product to be produced;
(b) product quality and quantity;
(c) the operational success of the product;
(d) training requirements for serving teachers and teacher-trainees;
(e) the impact of the programme on English language teaching and learning in Somalia in the light of the project objectives.

The place of evaluation in the project is outlined in Table A. Evaluation of current ELT practice in Somali schools has already determined the aims, objectives and mode of operation. At present (February 1982) we are in the production stage of Book 2. After a unit has been written and illustrated it is scrutinized by the whole team to ensure that the material is (a) linguistically appropriate and (b) methodologically appropriate, (c) culturally appropriate and (d) appropriate for the interests of secondary-school pupils. The unit is then revised in the light of the team's expert judgements. It is hoped that in this way quality control can be guaranteed. Although Book 1 was ready in June 1981, unpredicted technical reasons have delayed its printing. The printers have given assurances, however, that it will be ready for distribution by the end of February 1982 when it will be distributed to all secondary schools in Somalia. A full trial of Book 1 was not attempted as the team opted for immediate implementation in schools in view of the desperate shortage of materials and this, for the reason mentioned above, has not yet come about.

Book 2, however (and subsequent books yet to be written), will be trialled and the first half is now ready for duplication. It will be introduced into a small number of selected schools, urban and rural, in and around Mogadishu. The method to be utilized in evaluating this trialling are the same as those which will be employed to evaluate the final form of Books 1-4. The instruments are both formal and informal and will yield quantitative and qualitative data. The fully battery of instruments includes the following:

(a) Reports of observation by the Implementation Officer or other team member of classroom use of EFS. Such observation should give valuable data on the ability of teachers to use the material successfully and indicate areas in which in-service or pre-service training can improve the way in which it is taught. It will also assist in assessing pupil response to the course.

(b) A user's report filled in by each teacher will give data on the pace of teaching EFS and specific problem areas. It will also include an evaluation of each lesson by the teacher which should give an indication of his or her attitude to the new material.

(c) A questionnaire to be filled in on completion of the book or trial package. This will yield data on pupil motivation and teachers' attitudes to the teacher's notes and to the materials, and also indicate specific problem areas.

(d) A questionnaire to be filled in by the pupils so as to guage their reactions to the new course.

(e) Regular informal interviews with teachers will be a feature of the implementation/evaluation of the project. The questionnaires and reports will also be used as the bases for interviews.

(f) Student work will be sampled regularly as a means of evaluating their success in following the course.

(g) Tests in selected schools will be administered to students as another means of assessing the pedagogic success of the materials. Such tests will be based on the particular performance objectives of each book.

The data obtained from these instruments will be used

(a) to improve the production of subsequent books;

(b) to improve the provision of pre-service and in-service teacher training in order to augment the skills of the teaching cadre;

(c) to improve support for the teacher in terms of better teacher's notes and guides so that problems encountered can be overcome or circumvented;

(d) to assess the overall success of the project so as to inform projects of a similar nature elsewhere.

The role of evaluation is illustrated dynamically in Diagram A.

Operational Constraints

The following factors constrain the evaluation programme for EFS;

(a) The immediate pressing need for ELT materials in Somali schools means that there will be no time to trial Book 1, nor will there be any time to make major revisions of subsequent books. Trialling will thus

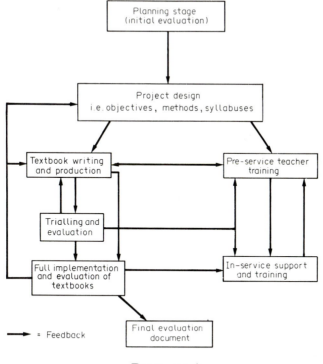

DIAGRAM A

serve as a means of identifying flaws which will not in all probability be corrected in the textbook; instead the emphasis will be on devising strategems for the teacher to cope with teaching difficulties which may be inherent in the materials.

(b) It will be difficult to monitor the progress of the books in the more remote schools because of the distances involved, poor communications and shortages of petrol. It is to be hoped that headmasters will be able to assist in the support of teachers in remoter areas.

(c) The chronic manpower shortage in Somali schools may mean that some classes will be untaught. Teacher absenteeism may also reduce the effectiveness of the course, although it is hoped that *EFS* can be used on a self-instructional basis.

The project is still very much in its infancy. *EFS* has not yet been introduced into any school and so the evaluation schemata for the textbook have still to be tried out. They too will be subject to evaluation, then to revision or rejection. The extent of the success of *EFS* will not be known for some time yet and that will be reported in another article.

TABLE A. *Evaluation in the Stages of EFS Project*

Stage	Evaluation instruments and methods
1. Determination of aims and objectives.	Needs analysis for English in Somalia based on consultation with Somali Ministry of Education, with head-masters and teachers, observation of teaching and student performance.
2. Planning, project design document, syllabus for each textbook.	As above.
3. Production.	To ensure quality control: *all* materials are evaluated by team both informally and formally in weekly plenary team meetings.
4. Trial.	Trialling is to be conducted in selected schools, urban and rural. Success is to be evaluated by means of observation, user's reports, questionnaires, discussion with teachers, samples of students' work and testing of student perform-ance.
5. Full implementation of final form.	Use of textbooks, teachers' notes and readers at national level. Success evaluated by means of observation, user's reports, discussion with teachers, samples of students' work and testing of student performance.

MATERIALS DESIGN FOR NIGERIAN SECONDARY SCHOOLS

NEVILLE J. H. GRANT

Free lance materials writer and consultant

'. . . the exercises we devise should aim at developing natural language behaviour.'

— Henry Widdowson

'He could not cope . . . the exercise. A up with B with C through D for'

— 'O' level language question

Introduction

In this paper, some of the problems involved in producing new English language-learning materials for Nigerian secondary schools will be discussed. The materials referred to have been published by Longman under the title *Secondary English Project*. The title of these materials is significant. At the outset, the writers were concerned that the exercise should not merely be one of writing materials: the intention was to attempt to work through a curriculum-development cycle, with field trials and feedback, so that users and potential users of the material — both teachers and students — would have considerable influence over their nature and format.

One of the main problems in any such exercise may be inferred from the juxtaposed quotations at the beginning of this paper. Our overriding concern was to try to develop materials which would enable the learners not just to manipulate the forms of language more or less accurately, but to communicate effectively. The central problem for any curriculum worker concerned with the teaching of language arts is that while his prime concern is naturally the learning of the language for genuine communication purposes, the teachers, the students, and indeed the examination system even, may often seem to place a higher premium on *usage* rather than *use*. This tends to be the case whether the language to French being learned in Britain, English being learnt in France, or English being learned in Nigeria. Quite simply, it is easier to teach, and to examine, *usage*, than it is to do the same with regard to *use*.[1] Our problem then was to teach both.

To begin with, we asked ourselves what the aims of teaching English in Nigerian secondary schools are — given that, at the time the project was initiated (1973), no definitive and generally accepted statement of such objectives had as far we knew ever appeared. In answering such a question, we clearly had to take account of the role of English in Nigeria, perhaps best summarized in an article by Bamgbose (1970):

> (English is) now the language of government, business and commerce, education the mass media, literature, and much internal as well as external communication. . . .
>
> (Spencer, 1971)

Bamgbose emphasizes the role of English in education:

> English is introduced as a subject in the first year of the primary school, and from the third year of the primary school up to and including the university level, it is the medium of instruction.[2] This in effect means that the Nigerian child's access to the cultural and scientific knowledge of the world is largely through English. . . .
>
> (Ibid.)

It is not surprising that many Nigerians feel ambivalent about this situation (Ubahakwe, 1980); but no one seriously questions that English has a very important role in Nigeria today, and will continue to do so for the forseeable future, especially in the field of education. It is clear, therefore, that in any formulation of the objectives of learning English at secondary level, the role of English in education should loom large.

1. Objectives of English at secondary level

It was decided that the following objectives should be our framework.

> (i) *To enable students to acquire sufficient proficiency in the four language skill areas of English to be able to progress as effectively as possible in all subjects in the school curriculum where English is required.*

In stating this objective, it was felt desirable to stress the fact that there are *four* skill areas, since speaking and listening skills tended to be widely neglected in Nigerian secondary schools, despite their importance in using the language as the medium of instruction. In training these skills, our main goal was information exchange, on subjects relevant to the curriculum, or to the students' interests, rather than the mere recognition and reproduction of elements of language—phonemes and the like—in a formal sense; though, inevitably, the latter had to play some part in the materials.

> (ii) *To enable students to acquire sufficient proficiency in the language to be able to learn, either formally or informally, in both the spoken and written modes, once they have left their secondary institutions.*

This highlights the concern that students should if possible reach a self-reliant 'take-off' stage by the end of their secondary education, if not before, particularly with regard to reading and study strategies.

(iii) *To enable students to communicate in all social situations in Nigeria in which English may be deemed necessary.*

The question-begging nature of this objective will be obvious. The fact is that unless and until the kind of socio-linguistic research documented by such workers as Scotton (1972, 1975) has been carried out with regard to the use of English in Nigeria, whatever insights one has on the question are bound to be largely a question of subjective judgement.

(iv) *To equip students with a brand of English which is both nationally acceptable, and internationally intelligible* (in Bamgbose's famous phrase).

The extent to which 'Nigerian English' — if an when it becomes defined — can or should be treated as an accepted variety of English is a recurring problem. The issue is particularly serious with regard to oral English (see, for example, Tiffen, 1974). Among Nigerian academics, Adeyanju (1981) appears to be almost alone in arguing for the use of RP as a teaching model; but many practising teachers, and examiners, would agree with him. Despite the well-known logistic problems involved, the West African Examinations Council has still not abandoned attempts to examine English orally at 'O' level, and an oral English examination is still compulsory for trainee teachers. In these examinations, RP is used as a model (if not the target — an important difference). Other authorities (Bamgbose, 1970; Ubahakwe, 1980) point out that the growth of Nigerian English is at least inevitable, if not desirable, and attempt to distinguish between acceptable variants — at lexical, syntactic and phonological levels — common among educated Nigerian speakers of English, and other variants that are unacceptable because they significantly impede communication.

(v) *To reinforce, so far as is necessary for and compatible with the foregoing, such cognitive, affective and psycho-motor processes as are thought necessary for an educated person by the designers of the total curriculum.*

This objective stresses the role that English, along with all other subjects on the timetable, must play in achieving the total goals of the curriculum, as defined, for example, in the Nigerian Educational Research Council Curriculum Conference of 1969.[3]

An NERC report of 1978 regrets the way in which subjects 'are too rigidly compartmentalized . . . it does not appear that there is enough correlation and integration between the efforts of one department and those of the others in the school.[4]

(vi) *To enable the students to pass the West African Examination Council's 'O' level English language examination.*

It is difficult to exaggerate the importance that this examination has for both teachers and students. Many examples can be cited of the undue influence that the terminal examination has on teaching and learning strategies even years before it is taken. Just one will suffice here:

Recently, the format of the 'O' level WAEC examination changed slightly: among the questions following the reading passage(s), is one 'requiring candidates to distinguish between phrase, clause, and sentence, and to recognize the grammatical function of words, phrases and clauses in their context.' This change reflected current feelings in Nigeria that formal grammar has been neglected for too long, and that it is this neglect that is the culprit for 'falling standards' in English.

The intention was to encourage teachers to introduce a certain amount of functional grammar into the classroom, and only about 2 per cent of the marks on one paper were likely to be affected. Yet the effect in some schools at last has been very marked: funds have been allocated to the purchase of books of traditional grammar, and many language lessons are in danger of becoming lectures in formal grammar.

2.   What kind of materials?

In trying to decide what kind of materials were most likely to achieve the objectives outline above, it was necessary to take into account a number of factors:

(i) The students. The main characteristic of secondary-school entrants in Nigeria is little different from that of any very large group of students anywhere in the world: diversity. However, with the enormous and rapid changes that have taken place in education in Nigeria – and particularly the huge expansion in education provision that was taking place even before the initiation of the Universal Primary Education (UPE) policy in 1976 – it is hard to exaggerate the diversity of Form 1 students in Nigeria, both educationally, culturally and linguistically. No one set of materials could possibly cater for all students beginning Form 1 in Nigeria – all one could hope to do was to devise materials that would at least be suitable for as wide a segment as possible. Even this could not be achieved unless the materials allowed for considerable flexibility in the way in which they were handled, by means of a variety of choice points built into the materials, and in particular in the Teachers' Notes. The last point was particularly important: our own research revealed that some Form 1 students were very nearly capable of passing the 'O' level WAEC examination within a year or so of starting secondary school; at the other end of the spectrum, there was a significant number who were functionally illiterate, and who, effectively, needed a complete beginner's course. Clearly, the same materials could not cater for both these extremes; we decided that we should not try to cater for either of these extremes, at least in the first phase of the project.[5]

(ii) The teachers. The teaching force is characterized by a similar diversity. Again, even before the advent of UPE, many schools suffered from a shortage of trained teachers. With the massive expansion of secondary education that has taken place this problem is likely to remain for a long time, despite attempts to make up for the shortage with crash courses and the development of NYSC (National Youth Service Corps) teachers.

A number of other problems existed: the teachers felt, and feel, that, as a group, they are not as socially valued (and paid) in the way they ought to be – and once were; and in consequence, morale is not as high as it ought to be. Nor, as it might be thought, is this a question merely of pay and promotion: where a state ministry of education actively encourages teachers to take a more professional interest in their work, by consultation, and by the provision of regional advisory centres where teachers can seek support and advice (rather than 'supervision' or 'inspection'), quite dramatic improvements can take place in the quality of education offered – at least as measured in terms of examination passes. The experience of Anambra State deserves study in this respect (Clement Agunwa, personal communication). It is also the experience of the authors that teachers who are asked to participate in workshops evaluating textbooks, respond in a most active and enthusiastic way, and often state that such exercises give them renewed enthusiasm for their job. In this respect we cannot agree with Sofenwa, who in lamenting the 'inadequate post-training or post-graduation development of teachers', accuses the latter of regarding 'their professional or academic qualifications as an eternal guarantee of competence and efficiency'.[6]

Because of the endemic 'diploma disease', teachers on the whole tend to be a conservative body, and tend, for quite understandable reasons, to see the sixth objective – that relating to the public examination – as the most important when judging new materials. Even those designed for the first year of secondary education, when the very important terminal examinations is still five or six years away, are judged with one eye on the format of this examination? In short, we felt that whatever materials were produced had to be sufficiently familiar in format and approach to avoid alienating teachers; but at the same time had to be sufficiently novel to effect the radical improvements in the quality of learning that were the project's objectives.

(iii) The syllabuses. Clearly, the materials produced had to be in tune with enlightened/official opinion, and should as far as possible accommodate whatever syllabuses had been officially laid down. It was evident from our meetings with teachers that in many cases, there was only one syllabus: that of the 'O' level examination – an examination syllabus. All too often teaching syllabuses especially for junior classes were almost wholly dictated by whatever textbook the teacher or school happened to be using.

Apart from the 'O' level examination syllabus, the syllabuses that were consulted when planning the course were:

Junior Post-Primary English Syllabus—Institute of Education, Ahmadu Bello University, Zaria, 1972.

A *Handbook for Secondary School Teachers of English* with syllabus and method guidelines for a Foundation Course in English at Junior Secondary Level—Western State Ministry of Education, Ibadan, 1974.

A *Syllabus for English at Secondary Level*—Curriculum Revision Unit, Institute of Education, University of Sierra Leone, 1974.

Guidelines on Nigerian Secondary Education English Curriculum—NERC. Federal Ministry of Information Printing Division, Lagos, 1978. (This document only became available at later stages in the project.)

In their different ways, these were all very valuable curriculum documents. However, as anyone who tries to map an official syllabus on to detailed learning materials will soon discover, and attempt to implement a given syllabus in complete detail is doomed to failure. The writers did not feel bound by any one syllabus in developing the materials, which was in the event just as well, since most of these syllabuses have in any case been overtaken by the swift pace of events: by the massive expansion in education that has taken place, and by the restructuring of Nigerian secondary education from a single-tier five-year structure, to a two-tier three-year plus three-year structure. No definitive syllabus for the new structure has yet emerged, at the time of writing (January 1982).

(iv) Financial. Materials have to be paid for, and funds for the purchase of materials are, of course, limited. It was clear that the materials produced should not be significantly more expensive than others on the market.

Taking into account all the factors briefly outline above, it was hard to escape the conclusion that a course book, or a group of course books, was what was required. Teachers are very much geared up to using one main course book, whatever other materials may also be used, and greatly rely on such a book when planning their work: as we have observed already, it is often the case that syllabus and course book are regarded as one. Given the extraordinary turnover and mobility of teachers, it is often the course book, rather than a stable teaching force, that gives the work in a school or class any kind of continuity.

The course book then would treat all areas of the English-language syllabus in a systematic way, and would integrate these areas as far as possible, such that the work in one aspect, e.g. reading skills, would dovetail in with that in other aspects, to make the language learning as efficient as possible. The course would try to use an 'activity' approach to language/learning, to maximize student participation. Attempts would be made to encourage student–student interaction, rather than the traditional teacher–student pattern that largely dominates so many classrooms.

At the same time, it was clear to us that the use of a main course book has a number of dangers, the most obvious of which is that teachers, especially those who are untrained, tend to teach the book, rather than the students. With many teachers, even those who are trained, the perceived needs of the book, rather than those of the students, tend to determine what is taught, and how it is taught.

Our central problem could, therefore, be summarized as follows: given that the teachers expected, and probably in many if not most cases, needed, a comprehensive, all-purpose textbook, how could such a book be designed in such a manner that it could become a flexible instrument for adaptation and use with a very wide variety of student and class? The problem is not an easy one, and we cannot claim to have solved it. But our attempted solution included the following strategies:

1. It was decided to try out the materials to determine whether, in fact, they *could* be used in a variety of different classes. A number of schools in different parts of Nigeria, as well as Ghana and Sierra Leone, took part in these trials, and a great deal of useful feedback was obtained. Much of the feedback at this stage concerned question validation — for example, detailed statistical information on Multiple Choice questions. While this was useful, the feedback obtained in the early stages of the project was of limited value, either because of the Hawthorne effect, or, on the contrary, because some teachers could not take seriously material that was not properly printed within the covers of a book. In fact, for a variety of reasons, the feedback that has been obtained after publication has been a great deal more valuable.

2. For every year of the course it was decided to provide a *Teacher's Guide* to give far more detailed advice and suggestions than has normally been the case in the past. Among the suggestions would be constant reminders to the teacher of ways in which the approach recommended could be adapted for differing classes.

3. In an attempt to cater for the inevitable situation where a teacher does not for one reason or another have a Teachers' Guide (problems of book purchase and supply in Nigeria could easily be made the subject of a separate paper), the Students' Book included to some extent at least a certain amount of incidental methodological guidance, so that, again, teachers could see that more than one possible approach was open to them in handling the text. Reactions to this have varied: some teachers resent some of the more overt 'instructions' contained in the Students' Book; but most have responded favourably.

4. We did not, and do not, know enough about the learning styles of the students to be able to come down in favour of any one theory of learning nor, in the writer's view, is any one theory of learning ever likely to be arrived at. However, all that we have ever managed to learn about theories of

learning, and the students, seemed to indicate that different people 'learn' the same things in different ways, and it seemed to us, therefore, that our methodology should be eclectic, to reflect both inductive and deductive learning styles. So in the teaching of grammar there is a mixture of 'cognitive code learning' for those with a deductive learning style, and 'pattern practice' for those who learn better inductively. However, as we have already indicated, the main thrust of our efforts was towards establishing communicative activity.

A typical grammar exercise, then, might consist of some formal grammatical explanation, either at the beginning or the end of a section, together with some kind of pattern practice, using a Matching table.

However, most of the section would be taken up with 'communication practice' of one kind or another. Thus for example, a section on Type 1 'If' clauses has a picture of Mr. Palaver hurtling down a hill towards a huge lorry parked across the road, and this kind of exercise:

Discuss these questions with your teacher:
1. What will happen if his brakes don't work?
2. What will happen if he crashes into the lorry?
3. What will happen if he breaks his leg?
4. What will happen if he is taken to hospital?
5. Who will visit him if he has to stay in hospital?
6. Who will help his family if he has to stay in hospital for a long time?
(*Secondary English Project Book 2*, page 52).

This kind of exercise may later be carried out by students working in pairs. These kinds of exercises are very far removed from the traditional language exercise that, for as long as anyone can remember, has always played an important part in language teaching classrooms. The traditional exercise requires students to work through a series of unrelated sentences, changing them or completing them in some way according to some grammatical rule that they have just 'learnt'. The students work through the exercises, nos. 1–10, 1–20, or even 1–30, individually, in writing; the exercise is then marked, and the marks entered in a mark book. The students have worked, the teachers have marked, the system is satisfied.*

Our concern was to get the more eclectic, and communicative, approach used in SEP into classrooms where the traditional language exercise still dominates, and we do not apologize, therefore, for giving a grammatical label ('*If* clauses' and the like) to sections containing such activities.

5. Most textbooks ask the teachers to 'provide extra remedial exercises for those students who require them'; but fail to supply either the means to identify those students who are in need, or the remedial exercises. In the *Secondary English Project*, we decided to supply these branches to the main programme. However, the problem remained as to what aspects of the syllabus should be isolated and tested in this manner?

It was known that teachers tended to see the class as the teaching unit, and it was not the norm for classes to be divided up into different groups. If too radical a branching programme was provided, many teachers might be put off by the complications that might ensue. However, all the teachers we consulted agreed that in most classes there was likely to be at least a minority of students who needed extra help in manipulating the basic structures of the language, and it was decided, therefore, to provide in the course regular diagnostic tests on key areas of syntax—usually a week or more after the topic has been treated. Those who need further assistance and practice are then referred to a corresponding revision exercise at the back of the book. These exercises can be used either as 'work cards' for individual students, or as materials for revision lessons to be given to some or all members of a class. This strategy meant that some of the more mundane exercises in *accuracy*—'usage'—did not need to clutter the main part of the textbook, which could thus focus more on *fluency*—'use'.[7] This strategy of providing a branching rather than a linear programme has proved extremely popular among those using the materials.

---

* The defects of such a procedure will be obvious: it emphasizes usage rather than use; accuracy rather than fluency, form rather than function. In its failure to deploy the target item in any kind of communication context, it must have played a major part in the failure of thousands, probably millions, of students to transfer what they do in the language classroom to what they may be required to do outside. Our own view was that while a certain amount of this manipulation practice may be necessary, it can never be sufficient: only with communication practice can there be any hope of transfer.

6. The materials include a number of 'enrichment' items not of central importance to the course, but to be used as optional 'extras' as required. These optional extras, often labelled 'On your own', include songs, poems, riddles, puzzles, and suggestions for further activities. Thus, for example, students might be invited to bring their own riddles into class. Many of the songs and poems are traditional Nigerian items translated from Nigerian languages, such as Yoruba, Igbo and Hausa, and students are encouraged to submit similar material of their own (in English of course) for the class to enjoy. Nigerians are justifiably proud of their rich cultural heritage, and such activities encourage the students to see English as a Nigerian language, rather than as a foreign language. (*pace* Ubahakwe, 1980, many Nigerians now see English as a Nigerian language.)

Teachers are encouraged to follow up such activities with ideas of their own. The optional 'loops' have had a significant affect on motivation and interest. In parenthesis, it could perhaps be added here that the role of literature in ESL teaching situations is, in the author's view, greatly underestimated by those who argue for more 'functional' approaches to language teaching. For example, here is a traditional praise-poem from the Igbo people of Nigeria, where wrestling is an important traditional pastime among Igbo speakers. The poem can be used in various ways in the classroom, for example, as reinforcement material following the teaching of the use of relative clauses:

> In praise of a hero
>
> Young man, you are:
> A hare that ascends a hill running
> A rope that drags the elephant along
> A lion that kills the leopard
> A head that never touches the ground
> A log of the *inyi* wood.
> (Egudu and Nwoga, 1973)

A reading and discussion of this poem can eventually lead to an exercise in creative writing. The students can be invited to write their own similar poem — either another praise poem, or perhaps even a mocking poem (another traditional genre). For example, their poems could begin:

> Lazy man, you are:
> A ..... that .....
> *or*   Beautiful maiden, you are:
> A ..... that .....
> *etc.*

7. By its very nature, the textbook tends to give undue prominence to the written word. To counter this, and to try to encourage oral activities, tapes have been prepared to go with the course. The tapes include songs and poems

as well as the more usual recognition exercises, drills and dialogues. Those who have heard the tapes respond very positively to them, despite the fact that they are not as cheap as the authors would like. (In some cases, teachers have paid for the tapes out of their own pockets, as funds for such audio-visual aids are not always easy to obtain.)

These tapes give much needed support to those teachers who recognize the importance of oracy in the English language classroom, and provide native-speaker models for students who might otherwise never experience them.

8. There is one more, obvious, way, in which one could hope to liberate teachers (and students) from the day-to-day full frontal exposure to one textbook, and that is by providing others. Some educators have experimented with the idea of providing separate books for each area of the syllabus, but in the writer's view such an approach suffers from several defects, the most important of which is that the principle of integration, whereby work in one area of the syllabus reinforces that in another, is no longer operative.

However, there is one specific area of the syllabus where it is really quite difficult for one textbook to provide adequate coverage, and that is in the area that we have called Applied Reading Skills; it is to this topic that we now briefly turn before bringing this paper to a close.

3. Applied Reading Skills

What in the Secondary English Project we call 'Applied Reading Skills' include access skills (how to locate books in a library; how to use reference books; how to find one's way round a book, using the contents page, the index, glossaries, etc.); skimming, or reading for gist; scanning, or reading for specific information; and the various strategies involved in efficient reading for study.

These skills are in practice often totally neglected in the English lesson, and indeed right across the curriculum, and as a result, it is far from uncommon to find students even at university who do not know how to find their way round a textbook, or who do not know any of the basic techniques of study.

There are many reasons for this neglect. One reason for this is well argued by Widdowson (1978). As he says, the 'reading passage' in a language course 'has something of the character of a display case. . . . passages of this kind function essentially as exemplification of linguistic elements . . .' and are thus to some extent at least a 'contrivance'. They may thus often be very different from 'authentic text'.[8]

The way such passages are treated, too, is not in general calculated to teach 'authentic', or 'realistic', response. There is, it is true, something very artificial about the usual kinds of 'comprehension question' that accompany such texts, which seldom seek to elicit any kind of authentic response. The hoops learners jump through at the behest of language teachers or examiners are very different from the obstacles they face in real life, when, for example, they may have to read a chapter of their history book for homework, or when, they have only ten minutes to revise Chapter 7 of their geography book ready for a test. The language teacher trains his students to comprehend, but 'in slow motion', often with nit-picking comprehension questions. The skills he is training seem to have little transfer value in real situations. Often such training is counter-productive: to require learners to spend half an hour reading a 500-word passage and answering ten comprehension questions is likely to develop in the students the kind of slow, meticulous reading style that will stand them in very bad stead in most real-life reading situations.

In the main course books of *Secondary English Project* some attempt is made to get away from the traditional comprehension passage, and the treatment that goes with it. There are some extracts that are not selected purely because they illustrate language-teaching points, but which are there because they are authentic and interesting in their own right. Some extracts are not accompanied by the battery of traditional comprehension questions. Many extracts are treated with the group discussion approach outlined in Munby (1968).

There are concerted attempts to get the students to tackle texts in a purposeful manner, with a survey 'read', and gist-type questions, and questions requiring authentic non-verbal responses, and so forth. But in general it must be admitted that the course has had to follow the language-teaching rules that those who use it expect it to follow: the course contains many comprehension passages with the kinds of question and activity that teachers, learners and examiners would expect of it.

'Applied Reading Skills' are treated mainly in *Reading for a Purpose* Books 1–3. These books were published as optional extras to the main course book, in an attempt to liberate the teaching of reading from its usual language-teaching mould.[9] They approach the teaching of reading from a 'real life' rather than a language-learning point of view. Students learn how to use a textbook — a contents page, an index, and so forth. We have found students — and teachers — nearly stunned at the idea that in using such a book, it is the reader, not the author, who 'calls the shots'. The reader can decide to read the last chapter first; to skip *this* chapter, to leave out *that* chapter until later, to read only the summaries of *those* chapters. That many books, most books, do not need to be read from cover to cover at all, but that one can locate those parts of a book relevant to one's purpose by using the contents page, or the index; that different books can be read in different ways, and at different speeds, depending on one's reading purposes: such ideas are completely new to many teachers, let alone students. This promotion of the reader, rather than the author, to be 'in charge' of a book is not by any means new to those who are brought up to regard books as the every-day furniture of their lives. But to those for whom books are precious and rare, expensive luxuries, very often to be shared one between three or more, such notions amount to heresy, and need to be introduced carefully, systematically, and gradually — in fact, in our experience over a period of years.

The series looks too at different kinds of reference books, and the various ways in which they can be used. It teaches students how to scan quickly to find out various items of information — each book has an index, and students typically have to find the 'passage' they need for a given exercise; the exercises are not traditional comprehension exercises; they are intended to arouse the students' curiosity, and then bring them to satisfy it by their own activities. 'Where is the biggest mango tree in the world?', 'When and where was Muhammad Ali born?' — these are questions that, once asked, need to be answered — by using applied reading skills.

This is not the time to attempt an exhaustive examination of the kinds of practical reading skill that *Reading for a Purpose* seeks to train, and other important aspects of the book — including study skills, notemaking, faster reading and so forth — can only be mentioned in passing. It may be asked 'Why were such crucial skills not included in the main course book?' There are many reasons for this. In the first place, some of these skills are given a fair amoung of treatment in *Secondary English Project* — but space simply did not allow them to be developed in the manner required. Had they been included in the quantity and manner we though necessary, the main course books would have become very large and unwieldy.

In addition, the Teacher's Notes for *Secondary English Project* recommend that only one class set of *Reading for a Purpose* should be obtained by a school: the books can then be issued out, and collected in again, at the beginning and end of one lesson each week. In this way, a single set can be used with more than one class, and the exercises — speed reading, information location, and so forth — are not invalidated by students reading them, out of interest, in advance. A further advantage is that *Reading for a Purpose* can be used in conjunction with any main course book.

4. Conclusion

There are many lessons we have learnt, and are still learning, from the exercise briefly described in this article. But perhaps the most important lesson of all is that the kind of curriculum development project described here stands little chance of success unless there is maximum involvement in the process at all stages. In a country as vast as Nigeria, it is often difficult to obtain as much detailed feedback as one would like, but the effort is well worth while.

In this exercise, the feedback, both positive and negative, obtained from the teachers in particular has proved invaluable, and we are grateful to the teachers, and their students, for making the project possible.

Notes

1. Widdowson (1978, Chapter 1) discusses the differences between *usage* and *use*.
2. It is now Federal Government policy that Nigerian languages should be the medium of instruction for at least the first three years of primary education.
3. These objectives are summarized on page 10 of the NERC document *Guidelines on Nigerian Secondary Education English Curriculum: a report of the English Curriculum Specialist Panel Workshop September 30th–October 4th 1974*; Federal Ministry of Information Printing Division Lagos, 1978.
4. *Ibid*, p. 10.
5. The first phase of the project was to produce a five-year English course, culminating in the 'O' level English-language examination. In the second phase of the project, which has just begun, we are obtaining feedback on this five-year course, and preparing materials to cater for the students at the lower end of the achievement range, namely the 'LINK' course (Grant and Omojuwa, forthcoming).
6. The same writer does, however, make some other interesting observations about 'the learning process in Nigerian schools'; *inter alia*, he remarks on the 'absolute faith in and preponderant reliance on textbooks by both the teachers and learners' and the 'short-cut and rapid results mentality of the Nigerian public which encourages students to insist that they are taught as narrowly as possible within the textbook'; 'the inadequacy of instructional facilities and materials in the great majority of schools'; 'the single-minded adherence to the prescriptions of the syllabi to the exclusion of other learning experiences'; and 'the understandable concern for passing external examinations' (Sofenwa, 1976). It is noteworthy that the writer made these complaints before the huge expansion and recognition of secondary schools that took place at the end of the decade as the full impact of the Federal Government's UPE policy became felt in the secondary schools.
7. For a discussion of 'fluency' versus 'accuracy', see Brumfit and Johnson (1979), pp. 187 *et seq*.
8. Widdowson, *op. cit.*, pp. 77 *et seq*.
9. The issues are discussed more fully in Lautamatti (1978).

References

ADEYANJU, THOMAS K. (1981) Is Nigerian English a realistic model to teach? Paper delivered at IATEFL Conference, London.

BAMGBOSE, AYO (1970) The English Language in Nigeria. In SPENCER (1970).

BRUMFIT, C. J. and JOHNSON, K. (1979) *The Communicative Approach to Language Teaching*. Oxford University Press, Oxford.

EGUDU, R. and NWOGA, D. (1979) *Igbo Traditional Verse*. Heinemann, London.

GRANT, NEVILLE J. H., OLAGOKE, D. OLU, and SOUTHERN, K. R. (1976, 1977) *Secondary English Project* Students' Books 1 and 2 (with Teacher's Books), Longman, London.

GRANT, NEVILLE J. H. and OLAGOKE, D. OLU (1978, 1979, 1980) *Secondary English Project* Students' Books 3, 4 and 5 (with Teachers' Books and tape) Longman, London.

GRANT, NEVILLE J. H. and UNOH, S. O. (1976, 1977) *Reading for a Purpose* Books 1 and 2. Longman, London.

GRANT, NEVILLE J. H. and BLOOR, A. M. (1978) *Reading for a Purpose* Book 3. Longman, London.

LAUTAMATTI, LIISA (1978) Developing materials for teaching reading comprehension in a foreign language In: *The Teaching of Comprehension*, ETIC Occasional Paper, The British Council, London.

MUNBY, J. L. (1968) *Read and Think*. Longman, London.

SCOTTON, CAROL MYERS (1972) *Choosing a lingua franca in an African Capital*. Linguistic Research, Inc., Edmonton.

SCOTTON, CAROL MYERS (1975) *Multilingualism in Lagos—what it means to the social scientist*. In: HERBERT, ROBERT K. (ed.) *Patterns in Language, Culture and Society: sub-Saharan Africa*. Ohio State University Working Papers in Linguistics, 19.78–90 (1975).

SOFENWA, L. A. (1976) Principles of language text-book production. Paper delivered at National Language Centre Language-Teaching Materials Production Workshop, Lagos.

SPENCER, JOHN (Ed.) (1971) *The English Language in West Africa*. Longman, London.

TIFFEN, BRIAN (1974) The intelligibility of Nigerian English. PhD Thesis, University of London.

UBAHAKWE, EBO (1980) The dilemma in teaching English in Nigeria as a language of international communication. In: *ELTJ* **34,** 2.

WIDDOWSON, H. G. (1978) *Teaching Language as Communication*. Oxford University Press, Oxford.

EVALUATION OF EDUCATIONAL PROJECTS, WITH SPECIAL REFERENCE TO ENGLISH LANGUAGE EDUCATION

PAULINE M. REA

University of Dar es Salaam, Tanzania

Introduction

The purpose of this paper is to discuss aspects of evaluation within the framework of an English language education project. 'Project' is interpreted here in its widest sense, encompassing the variety of different contexts which together create and serve an educational programme. The first sections of the paper discuss general principles of project design and evaluation and highlight two main phases, feasibility and implementation, and describe the role of evaluation with reference to both these phases. A crucial distinction is drawn between 'product'- and 'process'-oriented evaluation exercises. The next section of the paper isolates the area of student assessment and focuses on examineable courses where there is potential conflict between the internal requirements of the ELT practitioner and the external requirements of the university. In the final section, the paper takes up the issue of project counterparting, 'a cardinal feature' of the KELT Scheme of particular interest to projects in developing countries, and describes some of the problems which arise from an essentially product-oriented framework for the evaluation of the success of project localisation. Throughout, the discussion draws on first-hand experience of the recently established Communication Skills Unit, henceforth CSU, at the University of Dar es Salaam, Tanzania.

1. Background

The need to provide students at the University of Dar es Salaam with training in English has been felt for some considerable time. Concern has been expressed over the decline in standards of students' English proficiency and the negative washback effects this has on their ability to benefit from university courses of instruction conducted entirely through the medium of English. However, it was not until 1977[1] that it was agreed[2] that courses in Communication Skills should be implemented. The initiative to establish the CSU came from the Faculty of Arts and Social Sciences, and the Department of Foreign Languages and Linguistics[3] proposed ways in which students' communication skills might be improved. This led to the establishment of the CSU in late 1978.

2. The process of project design

Too frequently those responsible for language-teaching programmes restrict their evaluation procedures to the assessment of student performance and issues related to course design and materials production whereas, in practice, project development, curriculum development, and evaluation are mutually dependent. The success of an ELT project depends on far more than internal soundness of fit. Swales (1980) makes a core distinction between 'internal' and 'external' validity claiming that language-teaching programmes tend to have 'high internal validity (quality of materials, efficient intra-departmental efficiency . . .) but low external validity (isolation from the rest of the institution, failure to appreciate student study behaviour . . .)'. In a recent article, Mountford (1981) importantly details three concepts axiomatic to successful project design and development: time-boundedness, counter-parting, and levels of staffing. Additionally, he discusses the evaluation of language-learning materials within 'a curriculum context . . . conditioned by an organizational setting . . . as part of an institutional framework, with its own policy and resources'. There are two shortcomings to this otherwise every useful paper which addresses important issues of ELT project design. Firstly, there is an ambiguity over his use of 'curriculum context'. Does this refer to the context of the ELT curriculum, or does it extend to the wider context in which the ELT project operates? The interpretation of 'organizational setting' and 'institutional framework' is similarly ambiguous. Are these factors intrinsic or extrinsic to the language-teaching project? Turning to the concepts of time-boundedness, counterparting, and levels of staffing, these are clearly pivotal to the successful implementation and maintenance of ELT projects. My only quibble here is with Mountford's presentation of them as isolates, the role of which is unclearly specified in the overall planning process. In my view, it is essential to perceive the interdependence of these concepts as they are firmly embedded, to varying degrees, at every level in a comprehensive project design. These points are taken further in the discussion which follows.

For me, there are two prerequisites to the proper evaluation of any language-teaching operation. Firstly, one has to be clear on what is meant by the term 'evaluation'. Secondly, it is important to fully understand the role and position of the ELT project in relation to the wider educational context in which it operates. I begin with an analysis of the second prerequisite through which the parameters of evaluation can be more clearly and appropriately defined.

An understanding of the role and position of the language project implies decisions at three distinct levels which are summarized in Table 1.

Taking the factors (outermost box) which are extrinsic to the ELT project first, these require an informed and realistic understanding of the educational setting, mainly in terms of its needs and available resources

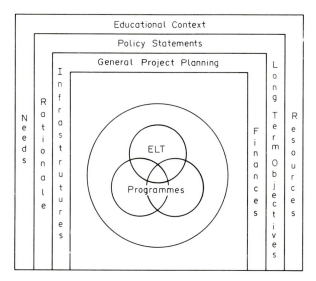

TABLE 1.   *Overview of the contexts of project planning*

(professional and support), which result in statements of a rather general nature. A higher degree of specificity is incorporated at the second stage (inner boxes) where, in some cases, individual institutions invite experts from outside to undertake a comprehensive feasibility study. There are many instances when, for example, the British Council has received specific requests of this kind. These studies then form the basis for recommendations for the implementation of an ELT project (University of Damascus, 1979; Petromin Vocational Training Centre, 1978; IUP Cuidad Guayana, 1977). In other cases, this responsibility falls to those appointed to the ELT posts which have been created on the basis of the initial fact-finding stage in the planning process (ELSU, University of Khartoum; CSU, University of Dar es Salaam; ELC, King Abdul Aziz University (KAAU), Saudi Arabia). In a well-planned operation the findings from this feasibility phase are interpreted in the form of a project design document, accompanied by a set of specific proposals leading to the implementation of an ELT curriculum. At this point statements of general policy are articulated, issues of project status are raised, together with a host of other considerations which include, crucially, forecasts of short- and long-term manpower requirements (local/expatriate, professional/support, full/part time), financial provisions, infrastructures, and channels of communication and accountability. These statements are offered within the framework of time-bounded project schedules. Specifically, they should illustrate (provisional) time-bounded short-, medium-, and longer-term objectives for the implementation of courses, and also integrate the notion of counterparting at both the pre- and post-training apprenticeship stages (see also final section of this paper on project localization).

At the end of this feasibility phase the first evaluation exercise takes place.

An obvious point perhaps, but if the project is to stand any chance of successful implementation, then the design document on which it is based should be discussed at various levels within the wider context of the institution as a whole, as well as with those at the ELT level of implementation. In other words, smooth and efficient running of the project depends on both internal and external support. Modifications and revisions are made to the blue-print, after which a final set of documents are submitted to the relevant authorities for approval and, hence, adoption as the project's working papers.

At this point in project design, the planner is brought to the interface between two contexts, that of the host institution on the one hand, and that of the narrower context of the ELT programme on the other. It is at this stage, then, when the initial detailed design documents have been accepted as the basis for the implementation of ELT courses that we move fairly and squarely into the domain of the language teaching operation, represented by the outer circle in Table 1. This in turn feeds into well-documented areas of syllabus design, followed by the actual production of language learning and teaching materials, and the provision of actual courses, represented by the inner circles in Table 1.

TABLE 2. *Evaluation and the project planning process*

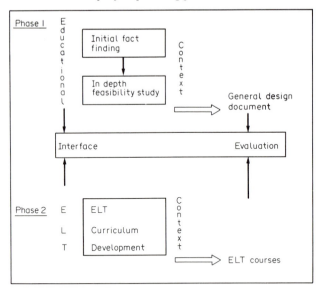

Two major phases have thus been identified in the project planning process, shown in Table 2. The initial, rather general definition of needs and resources is followed by a detailed and realistic planning phase which requires informed interpretation of all the available facts. Specific recommendations for the implementation of a project are explicitly stated after an in-depth feasibility survey. With these firm foundations laid by phase 1 in the form of a design document, considerations of ELT course design take over in phase 2. Unlike most models, I do not include evaluation as a final phase in the planning process. Whereas the feasibility and implementation phases follow sequentially, this cannot be said to be strictly the case with evaluation. Rather, evaluation should be regarded as firmly rooted from the start, with adequate provisions within the framework of the initial design documents (which I expand upon later). Further, evaluation cannot be restricted to the ELT domain alone, for the ELT operation exists to fulfil a function for specific sectors of the educational community at large, hence project 'success' can only be properly determined with reference to both the wider and narrower contexts described above, and is concerned with the extent to which both serve the needs of each other.

3. The role of evaluation within project design

Project evaluation is a multifaceted and very complex phenomenon. Yet it is so often assumed that evaluation means measurement, and that the object of this exercise should be that of student progress and achievement, on the basis of which claims of project success or failure are made. I do not deny the importance of monitoring student performance but, in answering the five questions in Table 3, I hope to show that in so restricting the concept of

TABLE 3. *Parameters of project evaluation*

EVALUATION

---

1. For *WHOM* is the information intended?
    (i) government, aid agencies, etc.
    (ii) host institution
    (iii) tutors
    (iv) students

2. What are the *PURPOSES* for evaluation?
    (i) information gathering and dissemination
    (ii) quality control
    (iii) accountability
    (iv) progress and achievement

3. To what *USE* will the information be put?
    (i) for information only
    (ii) decision-making leading to changes, modifications, etc.

4. Which *STRATEGIES* are to be used?
    (i) measurement
    (ii) self-assessment
    (iii) observation
    (iv) record/diary-keeping

5. What is the *TYPE* of information sought?
    (i) process
    (ii) product

---

evaluation other important areas and dimensions relevant to project evaluation are overlooked.

Firstly, different audiences need and expect information in different areas. For example, course tutors and materials writers will want to know about the strengths and weaknesses of the materials and the classroom methodology used. Those who produce materials will be particularly concerned with assessing the relevance of their materials for the target student population. Host institutions, on the other hand, will be more interested in the overall impact of the project within the context of the educational community and in the evaluation of student achievement. Where there are heavy expatriate involvements, they will wish to monitor the progress of the localization process and, together with government and other development agencies who have had significant financial interests in the project, they will be keen to receive information on the ways in which initial investment is to be safe-guarded and maintained.

These few examples are intended to show that different areas of evaluation are important to different people, at different times, and for different reasons. In some cases, the data elicited will be descriptive in nature and serve an explanatory function; in others it will be used as a basis for decision-making. At this point, it will be useful to recall the important distinctions between formative and summative assessment. The former serves as a feedback to participants in the evaluation *process*, and serves as a guide to future developments. Thus, project development and evaluation are inextricably interwoven in a process within which continuous developments and refinements are taking place. Hence, interests in project development are linked more closely with formative assessment and frequently, though by no means exclusively, will involve description rather than judgements and evaluations. Summative assessment, in contrast, is more concerned with *product*. The information is more likely to be quantitative in presentation and form the basis for decision-making. It follows from this that evaluation strategies will be diverse and that, in addition to formal measures such as standardized tests and university examinations, strategies of self-appraisal, interviews, and, importantly, observation are essential to any evaluation exercise. Moving away from the traditional model of reporting facts to the area of information exchange in the form of description implies, by definition, that the information presented will be more subjective. That this is the case does not, to my mind, diminish the validity of such information.

Before concluding this section, I wish to emphasize the importance of flexibility in project design and evaluation and to clarify the relative role and position of formative and summative assessment in the project-planning process. It should be obvious that detailed planning in the hands of the inexperienced can be damaging, and that rigidity in planning and slavish adherence to the adopted procedures is to be avoided. Any project design must have inherent flexibility, at every stage in the decision-making process, and machinery must exist to effectively monitor, over time, changed needs and circumstances. How is this to be achieved? Clearly, evaluation procedures must be built into project-design documents so that changes may be detected and responded to. However, it is not possible (nor desirable) to

TABLE 4.   *Formative and summative assessment as factors in project evaluation*

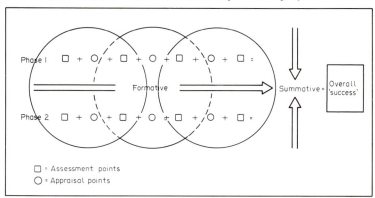

predict all the areas worthy of investigation. Thus, in addition to 'preordaining' specific check points in the design documents, there must be provision for an ongoing and developing evaluation process. Table 4 attempts to relate the notions of formative and summative assessment with reference to the feasibility and implementation phases of project design described earlier. The circles reflect the ongoing patterns of project development. The concepts of responsiveness and flexibility to changed circumstances are implicit within the notion of formative assessment and it is the sum of the information derived from the varied appraisal and assessment activities which leads, ultimately, to measures of overall success, or failure. Because of the evolutionary nature of an educational project and its curricula, it is important to observe what actually happens in the process of its development. Although some data will be prescriptive and evaluative, much of it, on account of the significant role of formative assessment in the evaluation process, will involve description. It is my view that the essence of project evaluation is 'responsive' evaluation and that whether the data is prescriptive or descriptive it results from the interaction of two contexts: the ELT context and the educational context within which it operates. To conclude, in the words of Stake (1972), 'it orients more directly to . . . activities than to intents . . . it responds to audience requirements for information'. The next section of the paper concentrates first on the conflicting interests of the ELT and the university contexts in the area of student assessment.

4.   Parameters of project evaluation: a case study

Student assessment

In the CSU, we are primarily concerned in helping students reach an adequate level in English communication skills for academic purposes and hence there is more emphasis in the programmes on formative assessment. However, in the case of examinable courses, there is potential conflict between the aims of the two contexts mentioned earlier. One of the problems which the CSU has encountered is in the area of coursework assessment, henceforth CWA. This is documented below with reference to CL100,[4] Communication Skills in English for first-year students in the Faculty of Arts and Social Sciences.

As background information, a high proportion of the total marks available is allocated to CWA:

CWA:	(i) assignments (accompanying course units)	— 40%	
	(ii) project (extended essay, *c.* 200 words)	— 20%	60%
EXAMINATION:			40%
			Total: 100

The distinction formative and summative assessment procedures in CL100 is as follows. When the outcome of an assignment is used as input for pedagogic purposes, then the assessment can be said to be formative. When the information is used mainly for classificatory purposes, then the assessment may be defined as summative. Conflicts arose at the implementation stage of this assessment philosophy.

On the one hand, the university requires CWA grades for student performance on the course. The university's purposes seem to be largely administrative and associated with the product of the learning process, namely (i) the maintenance and control of standards and (ii) student selection. On the other hand, CSU tutors need to be informed of the extent to which students have mastered the skills practised in the course. Their purposes are (i) to assess the process of learning, i.e. what changes are taking place during a course of instruction, and (ii) to identify areas of student weakness/strength so that suggestions for improvement and supplementary work may be made. Whereas university requirements may be classified as largely summative (terminal), formal, external to the learning process, and product oriented, CL100 course requirements are largely formative, diagnostic, and process oriented. Whereas the former requires a grade, the latter does not. Until recently, CL100 CWA assignments have been designed to satisfy these dual functions concurrently. The result has been that (i) the diagnostic and facilitating student-improvement objectives of the course have not always been fulfilled and (ii) coursework marks have not always matched the distribution pattern normally obtained by the university from student performance. Through experience, therefore, it is evident that a credit course design must integrate CWA methods and assignments to suit both the internal (ELT context) and external (university) purposes for student assessment and evaluation. The CL100 proposals are outlined in Table 5.

TABLE 5. *Internal and external CWA requirements*

Coursework assessment

A. *To satisfy the internal (pedagogic) requirements*, it is recommended that:
   1. Check points are integrated into the main stream of the course, in the form of tasks designed to determine:
      (a) whether the desired language behaviours/study skills have or have not been acquired, i.e. criterion-referenced tasks;
      (b) (in the case of inadequate performance) the extent to which these skills have been acquired so that appropriate remedial action may be implemented.
   2. Student performance at each of these check points be graded (not scored): Excellent, Good, Pass, Marginal Fail, Fail (this move should preempt student ill feeling when a score of 95% indicating near complete mastery, is not allowed to be carried forward as part of CWA).
   3. Further advice and supplementary practice activities should be made available for students who do not reach the acceptable pass standard.
   4. Students should be able to achieve full marks on tasks at these check points; tutors must therefore use the full range of grades available.
   5. Performance on repeat assignments will be assessed according to the full range of grades available.
   6. Any student who fails at a check point on two occasions should receive individual tutorial assistance; the course co-ordinator should be alerted at this stage.

B. *To satisfy the external (university) requirements*, it is recommended that:
   1. Four tests will be set:

TERM I	Test 1 — no earlier than 5th week of teaching (when students are settled into course)
	Test 2 — towards end of week 8 (allows time for corrections, advice, etc., before term ends)
TERM II	Test 3 — *c.* Week 4
	Test 4 — *c.* Week 8

   2. a Pass on a repeat assignment receives a C grade.
   3. 1 repeat performance only is allowed for; subsequent failure, a D/F grade is recorded.

These revised procedures will be implemented in the 1982/83 academic year and are the result of a gradual realization that the dual functions of coursework assessment cannot be served by uniform procedures.

Project localization

The second parameter I have selected, that of project localization, is more closely associated with university policy and with the interests of the external donor, namely the Overseas Development Administration (ODA) and the British Council (BC). Despite fullest support from all quarters within the university community and also from outside (Ministry of Education, Ministry of Manpower), the problems of recruiting local manpower have been constant throughout the Unit's development. If one adheres to the terms and conditions of the ODA/BC Kelt Scheme,[5] then the fact that the CSU is not self-reliant five years after the initial KELT input (1978) could reflect negatively in terms of project 'success' but, as I have already mentioned, success can only be determined with reference to both the wider educational contexts and the ELT context. In what follows, I identify the demands of the KELT Scheme on the CSU within the context of the University of Dar es Salaam, Tanzania, and document some of the problems associated with staffing that the Unit faces.

In Tanzania, there are very few English majors graduating from the University of Dar es Salaam (the only university in Tanzania). Firstly, the status of English in Tanzania has been lowered, largely because of the emphasis placed on the national language (Kiswahili) since Independence and, as a concomitant of this, the role of English with Tanzanian society is unclear and, often, misunderstood. Further, there are restricted job opportunities for English graduates. Apart from teaching which is itself a low-status (and unrewarding) profession, there are few other employment opportunities. Over the past five years, there have been approximately thirty English language graduates (majors)[6] from the University of Dar es Salaam, 20 per cent of whom graduated with an Upper Second or First Class degree. This constitutes a very small proportion indeed of the overall number of graduates from the Faculty of Arts and Social Sciences over the same period.

The general employment pattern of such graduates is placement in key positions in educational administration within the Ministry of National Education. As far as post-graduate training is concerned, there have only been six graduates at MA level in Linguistics with special reference to English since 1976, and there are no PhDs in this area.[7]

A further factor essential to judgements on the effective localization of the CSU project is the set of university requirements for the recruitment of academic members of staff, of which Table 6 is a summary.

TABLE 6.   *University recruitment requirements*

Qualifications[8]	.	Position
1. Good first degree (II[1] or 1) 2. Relevant teaching experience		Tutorial Assistant
3. MA		Assistant Lecturer/Lecturer
4. PhD		Senior Lecturer, and above

The University of Dar es Salaam has only recently celebrated its tenth anniversary and, from the facts on English majors described earlier, it is clear that no established cadre of trained Applied Linguists exists from which the CSU may draw its counterparts for senior positions, within the University staffing structure.[9] So far, the five counterparts recruited to the Unit have joined the University at the levels of tutorial assistant (three) and assistant lecturer (two). In addition to requirement 1 in Table 6, each has a diploma in the teaching of languages from a college of national education plus considerable teaching experience, ranging from five to ten years.

However, on joining the University, they have limited research and administrative experience. Given this profile, the CSU has organized a counterpart training programme, with three main phases:

1. *in-service (CSU) training*, including guided reading, assignments, teaching courses;
2. *MA/MSc training* (UK) in Applied English Linguistics;
3. *post-training apprenticeship*, on return to CSU, where gradually they assume a major responsibility for co-ordinating, writing, and teaching courses; for Unit administration and planning.

Present ODA/BC expectations are that by 1983 the CSU will have a Tanzanian Head with a team of qualified local staff. Table 7 presents an overview of the past, present, and future (at the moment of writing) staffing situation, and relates the process of counterparting to the three training phases above.

TABLE 7. *Overview of CSU staff trends*[11]

	78/79	79/80	80/81	81/82	82/83	83/84	84/85	85/86
Establishment[10]	2(?)	4(?)	10	10	10	10	10	10
Tanzanians:								
In-service at post	1	1	2	2	—	?	?	?
Training (UK)	—	1	1*	2	2	?	?	?
Post-training responsibility sharing	—	—	1	1	3	5	5	5
KELTS	2	4	4	6	5	3	—	—
Locally recruited staff, VSOs, post-graduate students from overseas, etc.	—	—	1	3	2	?	?	?
Staff present and teaching	3	5	7	11	10	8	5	5

* Overseas on 3-month Applied Linguistics course at Essex University.

The CSU teaching commitment is obviously constrained by the number of hours which can be realistically taught by the agreed establishment of ten. In addition, however, specialized manpower is still required for courses in the early stage of preparation, and for the supervision of counterparts in training. Further, there are other spheres of activity which, because of insufficient numbers of counterparts in the post-training apprenticeship phase, are handled entirely by expatriate members of staff. In view of the present decline in staff numbers, both KELT and locally recruited, and in the event of this present trend continuing,[12] then the consequences may be predicted as follows. It will be necessary to mobilize all available manpower for the teaching of the Unit's programmes and, as a result, other important activities will suffer. In this respect, the pre- and post-training phases are the areas most likely to be curtailed. It would be unwise to underestimate the impact of this on the Unit's development. Firstly, experience from the Department of Foreign Languages and Linguistics helps us here. Poor completion rates on overseas MA courses clearly indicates the need for rigorous in-service training in areas of Applied English linguistics prior to departure overseas. Secondly, from the profile of CSU staff members, it should be evident that a considerable amount of on-the-job experience may be required[13] before the stage is reached when counterparts may assume full responsibility for the effective and efficient running of the Unit, with facility and confidence, and with the support and acceptance of other members of the academic community ranging from members of the department to members of the University senate. These demands are high? Are they realistic? Or are they too high?

The description above of the CSU localization process serves the purposes of accountability and monitoring progress. It is intended mainly for the audiences of the host institution and the ODA/BC and will be used in decisions on maintaining staffing levels after 1984. It is presented in the form of a descriptive statement which is process rather than product (goal) oriented, concentrating less on achievements in relation to targets set in 1978 and rather more on the emerging needs and the different perspectives within the total context of staffing at the University of Dar es Salaam. Evaluative judgements on the basis of figures alone are, obviously, inadequate. Indeed the fact that only five counterparts have been recruited to the Unit since 1978 is grossly misleading, in view of the weakened tradition of expertise in English coupled with the urgent manpower needs for English specialists in other sectors of the country's educational system. The KELT Scheme at the University of Dar es Salaam has already been extended beyond the five-year pattern, with two additional Cadre KELT inputs in 1981, in response to emerging requirements. Nonetheless, it is on record that the recruitment of counterparts got off to a slow start, that the localization process is taking too long, and that the main responsibility for running the Unit should be in the hands of the Tanzanians by the 1983/84 academic year.

If one is to assess the success of the CSU's localization record to date on the basis of the aims, objectives, and timescales of the initial design document, then it has clearly failed. If, on the other hand, the concept of process and responsive evaluation is evoked, then it has undoubtedly scored successes in recruitment, in view of the prevailing levels of English language expertise in the country. It is indeed unfortunate that the possibilities of attracting and keeping locally recruited expatriate staff are rapidly decreasing at the time when the major KELT withdrawal is due to take effect. Although there will be five Tanzanians in the post-training phase by October 1983, this is insufficient to 'maintain progress towards agreed objectives' and 'to maintain operations at the level of attained objectives'[14] and thus the need for continuation for a shorter time scale of non-cadre posts (in an advisory capacity) and, for a longer time scale, the continuation of cadre posts, beyond the presently agreed limits of the project.

Conclusion

In the first part of this paper, I distinguished between two methods of reporting information from an evaluation exercise. One is concerned with the presentation of evidence, largely on the basis of objective measurement, whilst the second, more concerned with observation and objective reporting of relevant variables, is presented in the form of a detailed descriptive statement. Because of the current weighting in the literature towards product-oriented measurement reports, I have concentrated in this paper on process evaluation through descriptive reporting. Estimating project success is problematic. What constitutes success for one party may well be quite insignificant to the concerns of another. However, in all assessment and evaluation undertakings it is important to recognize contributions from a variety of different contexts. The two areas described in this paper have illustrated how the goals of these different contexts may conflict with each other and thus flexibility and responsiveness are crucial concepts in project development and evaluation. To my mind, the major impediment to effective development and evaluation arises when one is bound by product-oriented evaluation exercises, especially when their aims and objectives are linked to timescales specified at the outset of a project's development.

Notes

1. At around the same time, the idea of a university-wide teaching and learning programme was being considered, and in June 1978 the University Teaching and Learning Improvement Programme was established.
2. 64th Meeting of Senate, November 1977.
3. The head of department at this time, Dr J. St. C. Higham, was particularly instrumental in the early decision-making stages prior to the establishment of the CSU.
4. Although the problem described exists across CSU examinable courses, there is not a common CSU strategy across all courses.
5. 'It is a cardinal feature of the Scheme that the recipient government/institution should provide counterparts to take over as soon as is practicable from the British Staff provided. . . . The life of a post will not normally be longer than five years.' KELT Circular, Appendix A, The British Council, February 1977.
6. Personal communication from Hugh Trappes Lomax, Co-ordinator of the English Section, Department of Foreign Languages and Linguistics.
7. But PhD dissertations, in areas of Applied English Linguistics, are in preparation by two staff members of the Department of Foreign Languages and Linguistics.
8. I exclude here other additional requirements concerning number of publications, satisfactory teaching record, etc.
9. This is in sharp contrast to the contexts of the well-documented projects with a KELT involvement at the University of Malaysia and the University of Bogota, Los Andes.
10. Full Unit establishment was agreed after it had been in operation for eighteen months, i.e. in 1980.
11. This table indicates the level of KELT involvement as currently conceived.

12. This is likely to be the case because of the difficulty the University has in recruiting well-qualified expatriate staff because of its unattractive terms and conditions.
13. For example, negotiating course registration regulations and syllabus changes at Faculty Board levels, Unit administration, pursuing issues of staff recruitment, continuing the staff training programme for incoming Tanzanian staff members, and so on.
14. *Report of the Working Group on the KELT Scheme*, The British Council, p. 5, 1980.

References

MOUNTFORD, A. *Design, Evaluation and Testing in English Language Projects.* English Language Services Department, The British Council, London, July 1981.

STAKE, R. E. (1967) Toward a technology for the evaluation of educational programs. In: *Perspectives of Curriculum Evaluation*, Area Monograph Series on Curriculum Evaluation, No. 1, pp. 1–12.

SWALES, J. (1980) The educational environment and its relevance to ESP programme design. In: *Projects in Materials Design*, ELT documents Special, pp. 61–70, The British Council.

PROJECT PLANNING AND PERFORMANCE
Some thoughts on the efficiency and effectiveness of curriculum development projects; with a case study of the Centre for Developing English Language Teaching, Ain Shams University, Cairo

ROGER BOWERS

CDELT Ain Shams/The British Council

Introduction

The last twenty years have seen, in Africa as elsewhere, a large number of aid-supported curriculum development projects in teaching English as a second or foreign language. Some of these have been extensively reported, others less so. It is common to find at the end of such projects a shared sense of both achievement and under-achievement: while much has been done, much remains to be done, and the outcome of a project is never precisely what was predicted at its inception.

This paper explores reasons for the mismatch of project *planning* and project *performance*. It does so in three stages. First, a model is presented of the systems which are affected by any curriculum-development project and the critical factors which may in turn affect efficiency and effectiveness of performance. Secondly, these factors are exemplified through a single case study—the programmes of the Centre for Developing English Language Teaching (CDELT), Ain Shams University, Cairo, Arab Republic of Egypt. Finally, discussion centres on the avoidable and unavoidable, the positive and the negative aspects of project evolution. Some suggestions are made for ensuring maximum efficiency and effectiveness in projects.

A final word of introduction. The intention of this paper demands a fully objective statement and exemplification of project execution and achievement. Some of the judgements which I offer may appear less than congratulatory: it is a compliment to all concerned with CDELT that I feel able to make such judgements public in this form.[1]

I. Curriculum development projects: a model

At first sight every curriculum-development project is different, in almost every respect: in context, in aims, in time-scale, in resources, in institutional involvement, in personal style, in documentation, in achievement. Certainly, the project literature provides a rich and varied diet.[2]

In essence, however, any curriculum-development project may be seen as an attempt to initiate change in a common set of interlocking professional and administrative systems. Different projects, built on different principles of curriculum development, will initiate such change at a different point in the overall system, but change at any point in it implies change at every point. I wish in this section to describe the set of systems which curriculum innovation affects, and to define the issues which arise in each. These issues must be taken into account in *planning* a project. They will inevitably, as reactions to the project's primary action, shape a project's evolution and control its *performance*.

Diagram 1 summarizes the systems which interlock in any curriculum-development programme — the 'spider's web' which is set vibrating by the attempt to touch it at any point.

The classic distinction in curriculum innovation is that between initiation of change through PERSONNEL (boxes 1–3) and initiation of change through FACILITIES (boxes 4–6). Even this major dichotomy, however, indicates how inevitably interdependent the component systems are. We may begin our exploration of this interdependence by focusing on each system in turn and summarizing the issues raised in them.

Personnel

1.   Serving teachers

1.1. Will the programme affect all serving teachers, or only some?
1.2. Will career prospects be enhanced?
1.3. Are all serving teachers at the same initial behavioural level?
1.4. Will there be changes in staffing formulae, i.e. more specialist teachers?
1.5. Will there be changes in staff-student ratios?
1.6. Will teachers be withdrawn from service for training, either short term or long term?
1.7. Will teacher workloads be affected?
1.8. Will teachers share project management responsibility?

2.   Teacher trainers

2.1. Will programmes affect all teacher trainers or only some?
2.2. Will career prospects be enhanced?
2.3. Are all serving trainers at the same initial behavioural level?
2.4. Will there be changes in training staff formulae, e.g. more specialist trainers?
2.5. Will there be changes in trainer/trainee ratios?
2.6. Will trainer staff be withdrawn from service for upgrading, either short term or long term?
2.7. Will trainer workloads be affected?
2.8. Will trainers share in project management responsibility?

3.   Training programmes

3.1. Will there be courses for all serving teachers?
3.2. Will there be courses for specialist teachers?
3.3. Will there be courses for all trainers?
3.4. Will there be courses for specialist trainers?
3.5. Will there be courses for supervisors/inspectors?
3.6. Will existing courses be extended, or will new courses be developed?
3.7. Will the introduction of new courses require the abandonment of old courses?
3.8. Will training be intensified (causing a smaller throughput) or expanded (an increased throughput) or simply renovated (no change to throughput)?

DIAGRAM 1. *Interlocking systems affected by a curriculum development*

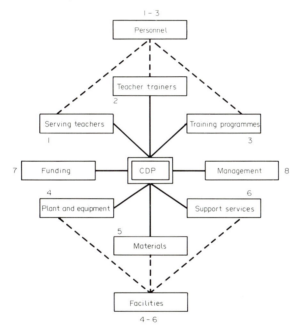

Facilities

4.   Plant and equipment

4.1. Will existing premises be modified, or extended?
4.2. Will new hardware be involved?
4.3. Will new software be involved?
4.4. Will storage and servicing facilities be expanded?
4.5. Will staff facilities be improved?

5.   Materials

5.1. Will existing teaching materials be revised?

5.2. Will existing teaching materials be supplemented?
5.3. Will existing teaching materials be replaced?
5.4. Will existing training materials be revised?
5.5. Will existing training materials be supplemented?
5.6. Will existing training materials be replaced?

6. Support services

6.1. Will existing support staff be trained?
6.2. Will support staff be expanded?
6.3. Will there be familiarization programmes for administrative staff (including principals, inspectors)?
6.4. Will administrative personnel be expanded?
6.5. Will curriculum development institutions/networks be established?
6.6. Will administrative workloads be affected?
6.7. Will administrative systems be affected, including chains of supply and of responsibility?
6.8. Will evaluation systems be affected, including examinations and personnel assessments?
6.9. Will administrative staff share in project management responsibility?

Funding

7.1. Will expenditure in any sector be increased?
7.2. Who during and after the project, will meet expenditure in the following sectors:
      serving teachers,
      teacher trainers,
      training courses,
      plant and equipment,
      materials,
      support services,
      management?
7.3. Will additional revenue be generated?
7.4. Who will receive such revenue, during and after the project?
7.5. Will individual emoluments and incentives be received?
7.6. Who will receive such payments during and after the project?
7.7. Will project costs curtail expenditure elsewhere?

Management

8.1. Where did the initiative for the project originate?
8.2. Who will carry overall project responsibility?
8.3. Who will carry overall financial responsibility?
8.4. Who will authorise project aims?
8.5. Who will appoint and be responsible for project staff?
8.6. Who will evaluate project achievement?

8.7. Who will terminate the project?

8.8. Who will be responsible for post-project programmes?

The issues raised above, are, it will be noted, more administrative or managerial than they are academic or professional. They are, however, critical, and they follow automatically from any 'professional' initiative. They are, moreover, closely interlinked. Not only every main heading 1–8, but possibly every sub-question (there are 59) is interdependent. The nature of these connections can be indicated through some obvious, and some less obvious, examples.

II. Testing the model

We may begin by showing how one block of questions — one general starting-point — affects other blocks.

Example 1

Block 1, within the area of PERSONNEL, is concerned with *serving teachers*. We may thus begin a curriculum project with the primary intention of 'upgrading the skills of serving teachers'. Any strategy to achieve this aim will raise all the questions in block 1: it will also raise questions in all other blocks, particularly blocks 2, 3, 6, 7, 8. From the outset, therefore, account must be taken of questions regarding *teacher trainers, training programmes, support services, funding and management*. We shall be less necessarily concerned with questions of *plant and equipment* and of *materials*.

Example 2

Still in the area of PERSONNEL, we may start in block 3 with recognition of the primary need 'to improve the scope and quality of *training programmes*'. Such an initiative has extensive implications for blocks 4, 5, 6, 7, 8: that is, for *plant and equipment, materials, support services, funding* and *management*. To ignore any of these areas is to run the risk that new programmes be internally well designed but in practice poorly implemented.

Example 3

We decide to tackle FACILITIES by 'improving the quality of *materials in use*': that is, our starting-point is block 5. But there are immediate and important implications for blocks 6, 7 and 8: that is, for *support services, funding* and *management*.

The set of implications stemming from a single starting-point is, as these examples indicate, complex. Indeed, both cumulative and backward implications have also to be accounted for. In other words, a block 1 starting-point (serving teachers) with a block 3 implication (training programmes) will accumulate all the implications of a block 3 activity; a block 5 (materials in use) starting-point may concern serving teachers and thus bring into play block 1 and all its implications.

There are thus few cases where a curriculum innovation centred on one of the sectors in Diagram 1 does not have a potential impact on all the other sectors. Wherever the 'spider's web' is touched, the whole trembles. Such interdependence cannot be fully catered for in project planning, or the objectives of a project would be limitless: but it is essential for every project to be fully aware of and conditioned by its effect upon other sectors. *Such effects are not only possible constraints upon current achievement but also the key to future progress.*

The effect of block upon block is, however, a generalization from the effect of an individual issue upon other specific issues. We may now consider some examples of the effect of specific question upon question, both within and between blocks.

Example 4

    1.1⟶ 1.2.

    1.1. Will the programme affect all serving teachers or only some?
    1.2. Will career prospects be enhanced?

A programme is envisaged in which, for financial reasons, only 20 per cent of teachers can be upgraded. This improves the career prospects of the 20 per cent beyond those of the majority. On the one hand, enhancement of prospects is a necessary and desirable incentive for upgrading. On the other hand, the programme divides the profession into an élite and a majority, which is detrimental to the profession as a whole and also politically unacceptable. Problems!

Example 5

    4.2 ⟶ 4.3.

    4.2 Will new hardware be involved?
    4.3 Will new software be involved?

A programme is launched to provide regional resource centres with audiovisual facilities. But inadequate provision is made for the ongoing supply of suitably designed materials. Problems!

Example 6

    5.1 ⟶ 5.4.

    5.1. Will existing teaching materials be revised?
    5.4. Will existing training materials be revised?

A programme is mounted to stimulate new classroom activities by revising fully the materials used in secondary schools. But the training materials used in the pre-service sector are not revised. So new teachers enter the profession trained in obsolete skills for obsolete materials. Problems!

Example 7

1.5 ⟶ 2.5 ⟶ 3.5 ⟶ 4.1 ⟶ 5.1 ⟶ 6.6 ⟶ 7.2 ⟶ 8.6.

1.5. Will there be changes in staff/student ratios?
2.5. Will there be changes in trainer/trainee ratios?
3.5. Will there be courses for supervisors/inspectors?
4.1. Will existing premises be modified, or extended?
5.1. Will existing materials be revised?
6.6. Will administrative workloads be affected?
7.2. Who will meet expenditure in the various sectors?
8.6. Who will evaluate project achievement?

A project aims to reduce primary-school class size as being the single major determinant of student achievement. But can trainers teach small-group techniques effectively when the trainer/trainee ratios themselves are unsatisfactory? Will inspectors assess appropriately a new intake of teachers trained in different techniques? Since the number of students in the system is unchanged, will students be accommodated in new classrooms or through an extended shift system? Since groups will be smaller, will materials be revised to encourage the new techniques now possible? Since more classes are involved, how much more complex will administration become—at school, district and national levels? Since more teachers and support staff will be needed, who will meet the extra cost now and later? Since different things will be happening in the classrooms, who will develop new evaluation measures and on the basis of these assess the measure of success achieved by the project? Problems!

Example 8

4.1 ⟶ 4.5 ⟶ 6.2 ⟶ 6.6 ⟶ 7.2 ⟶ 7.7 ⟶ 8.5 ⟶ 8.8.

4.1. Will existing premises be modified or expanded?
4.5. Will staff facilities be improved?
6.2. Will support staff be expanded?
6.6. Will administrative workloads be affected?
7.2. Who will meet expenditure, now and later?
7.7. Will project costs curtail expenditure elsewhere?
8.5. Who will appoint and be responsible for project staff?
8.8. Who will be responsible for post-project programmes?

A training institution decides to extend its overcrowded premises. The extension is designed for use as student classrooms, so the staff complain because their facilities remain inadequate. Cleaning staff complain because more rooms mean more work. Administrative staff complain because of extra work during construction and extra responsibilities (e.g. security) afterwards. The audiovisual unit complains because its plans for a new language laboratory were not given priority. The development work proves troublesome because the contractors report to the administration, not to the academic head, and insufficient account has been taken of design factors. The new rooms deteriorate because insufficient provision has been made centrally for their upkeep and the departmental head has no funds at his direct disposal. Problems!

These examples show simple chains of implication: they illustrate problems in small projects, problems so obvious that they might be thought not to occur in reality. But they do; they have. My own experience of working in projects, designing and evaluating them, or viewing them in passing, has offered many instances.

Yet the above examples are simplifications. A moment's thought will show the multiplicity of implications which inevitably apply whenever and wherever we initiate the process of change. (O what a tangled web we weave, when first we practise to achieve. . . .) It is not always that such questions go unnoticed: it is frequently the case that the planning phase of a project allows insufficient time to become aware of the pitfalls ahead and reach agreements on how to circumvent them.

Do such questions always receive study at the end of a project, then, when the problems which have been met – and, one hopes, solved – highlight questions which were not asked early enough or consequences which were not fully predicted? Unfortunately not. It is rare to find a fully objective and insightful evaluation of project performance measured against project plans, for reasons well discussed in Lawton (1978). And it is worth remembering – a note of encouragement – that *projects can overachieve as well as underachieve*; just as it is possible for negative side-effects to evade prediction so it is possible for positive implications to pass unnoticed and in the final evaluation be ignored or undervalued. Many projects may miss their primary targets and yet generate highly successful subsidiary activity and development.

But it is dangerous to indulge for too long in generalities. Readers will have counter-examples to cite of fully successful projects, accurate predictions, comprehensive evaluations – though I believe they will also have substantial evidence for the gaps between *planning* and *performance* which we have begun to consider. To exemplify in detail the relationship between project design and accomplishment, we shall now examine the Ain Shams CDELT project 1976/82. This case study will reveal a project which, like most, has both intended and unintended achievements to its credit and some disappointments. In comparing what was planned with what was performed, we shall attempt to identify the issues within our interlocking systems which explain the mismatch.

III. A case study: CDELT Ain Shams 1976–82

The background

1. The University

Ain Shams University is one of the major Egyptian universities. It was established in 1950 through the coalition, expansion and upgrading of existing institutions for academic study and teacher training. The university consists of ten faculties—Arts, Law, Commerce, Science, Medicine, Engineering, Agriculture, Education, Languages and the Women's College. The total student population in 1980 exceeded 100,000. The Faculty of Education is the oldest education faculty in Egypt, with a current student population of over 10,000 and over 1000 teaching staff.

2. The Centre for Developing English Language Teaching (CDELT)

In 1974 a Joint Working Group on US/Egypt collaboration recommended assistance to the language-training programmes of Ain Shams Faculty of Education 'with initial emphasis given to the training of Egyptian teachers of English'. Following consultations between the University and the University of California at Los Angeles, plans and programmes were drawn up for a Centre for Developing English Language Teaching to be situated within the Faculty of Education. Its primary aim was to provide high-level training in TEFL. Egyptian staff were selected for doctorate training at US universities while American staff undertook teaching duties at CDELT and assisted in the development of graduate programmes in TEFL designed with the assistance of senior UCLA personnel. A five-year collaborative programme was envisaged.

The planning year 1975/76 clarified objectives. Postgraduate training schemes comprised a one-year Diploma and a one-year MA in TEFL. The possibility of revision in the undergraduate curriculum in the Faculty of Education was discussed. It was suggested that the Centre might have some involvement in in-service training programmes and in a survey and analysis of national language training needs. The Centre became an established part of the University of Ain Shams under by-law in 1976.

At the same time, British involvement in TEFL at the Faculty of Education continued through the provision of contract teachers to the English Section of the Department of Modern Languages. The incumbents of these posts worked alongside the American CDELT team, and when in 1978 the British support was 'projectized' under the KELT (Key English Language Teaching) scheme administered by the British Council on behalf of the Overseas

Development Administration, account was taken of CDELT developments and priorities. By 1980 the British and American teams were working in close collaboration on Centre programmes within the Faculty.

3. The present situation

Currently CDELT receives support from a number of sources. Ain Shams as the host institution supplies premises, part-time staff and overall policy through a Governing Body, a part-time Director (Dean of the Faculty of Education) and a part-time Deputy Director. A team of four American staff is appointed through UCLA and managed in collaboration with USICA and the Fulbright Commission. A team of four British personnel is provided through the British Council by the Overseas Development Administration. There is joint team leadership and accountability. Project funding relies heavily on the support of the US Agency for International Development (USAID).

Working alongside part-time Egyptian staff, the team is currently engaged in:

- undergraduate curriculum revision;
- postgraduate TEFL training;
- test development;
- conference and seminar organization;
- research activity.

4. The future

As this paper is written, the future of the Centre is not clear. The University authorities must decide whether CDELT is the most effective means of achieving the aims originally specified and thus merits increased financial and personnel support. The aid agencies must subsequently decide what level of external support is appropriate at this stage of the Centre's development. A revised three-year development programme for 1982/85, agreed in principle, depends upon these support decisions.

The case study which follows thus reviews the initial aims of CDELT and the extent to which these have been achieved during the first phase of CDELT support and development. To what extent has performance matched planned intention?

IV. Review of factors affecting achievement

Some CDELT programmes may now be viewed in terms of their primary targets, with reference back to Diagram 1.

No CDELT programme has yet focused specifically on the needs of *serving teachers* (block 1).

THE PROGRAMMES

Six areas of activity will be reviewed. In each case, the area will be displayed in terms of three questions:

Planning What was the original intention?	*Performance* What was actually achieved?	*Interpretation* What explains the under- and over-achievements?
Undergraduate Curriculum Revision for Faculties of Education		
The initial proposal (1977) was for a set of materials to be used in Ain Shams Faculty of Education to assist teaching of all the language and literature components of the first- and second-year course.	The outcome of four years' team work is a set of eight student and teacher texts, with recorded tapes, covering the four *language* components of the first and second years. The course is to be published in 1982 as a University Course in English for Egypt. The pilot edition is in use in five other universities but not at Ain Shams.	The initial terms of reference for this project did not specify in detail the eventual scope of piloting and use. The scale of commitment to the project, the general validity of the materials, and withdrawal of the Ain Shams Faculty from the project all led to more widespread use of the materials than was originally intended. At the same time, a negative evaluation of the literature materials produced led to a reduction in the scope of the materials. The course now nearing completion is expected to find widespread use in the university sector, mostly within Faculties of Education, and to contribute to language upgrading in the first two years of the university curriculum. Associated orientation programmes have initiated junior staff improvement and may lead to more extensive training activity. There is now a demand for attention to the third- and fourth- year curriculum, especially in the 'outreach' universities.
Postgraduate Training Programmes		
The Professional Diploma was intended as an annual course for university junior	The Diploma ran from 1976/77 to 1979/80, training in all some 50 candidates. These	The postgraduate courses have under-achieved in numbers for administrative

THE PROGRAMMES (continued)

Planning What was the original intention?	*Performance* What was actually achieved?	*Interpretation* What explains the under- and over-achievements?
staff intending to proceed to MA level training, with 15/20 candidates per annum. The MA in EFL was intended to provide fully qualified staff for the faculties, plus some highly qualified staff for ministry posts.	came increasingly from Ministry (and Cairo) rather than from faculty backgrounds. In 1980 the Ministry withdrew study leave facilities for MA studies. The Diploma recommended in 1981/82, specifically for Ministry candidates as a terminal course for trainers and supervisors. The MA ran from 1977/78 to 1980/81. With no Diploma intake to draw on, the MA was in abeyance in 1981/82. Some 50 candidates completed the MA coursework and have completed or are working on their research theses.	reasons. The target population, not fully defined in the outset, was offered inadequate incentives to undertake CDELT courses rather than qualify through less demanding locally available programmes. The equivalence of the CDELT qualifications is still at issue, and with doubts over the freedom to proceed subsequently to PhD studies good candidates are understandably reluctant to commit themselves. In academic terms, however, the courses show considerable achievement. The taught courses are of a high standard. The theses are relevant and of a generally high quality. CDELT graduates have contributed to developments in TEFL through, for example, the Ministry's testing project and the National Council for Educational Research. More recently, the need to emphasize at the Diploma level more practical requirements has led to the production of courses in training, supervision and counselling techniques on a discourse basis which are innovatory within Egypt. Current proposals are for Diploma training to continue, for MA activity to take the revised form of Summer Institutes for MA candidates at any university, and for the Centre MA to be revived when equivalence matters are finally resolved.

English for Special Purposes Curriculum Development

At the request of the Faculty of Education, a two-year course was prepared for non-specialist students of English in the Faculty. The intention was to produce materials which could be used in unsatisfactory circumstances (few hours, large classes, poor motivation) by untrained junior staff.

Over a three-year period a print and tape course was prepared and fully trialled within the Faculty of Education. Junior staff shared in the preparation and trialling and received additional training through CDELT postgraduate programmes and summer institutes. Research was undertaken into the effectiveness of the materials, which were developed on a decoding-based rationale.

In 1981 the Faculty took the decision to cease use of the materials. No reasons were given. An outreach programme had not then been established, and the materials (not now in use) await final revision and publication.

The achievement of this programme lies chiefly in the process rather than in the use made (so far) of the product. The materials production project provided the basis for very close collaboration and effective task-related training. The materials themselves did not reach final form before the project was terminated through a decision made outside the Centre. They are, however, in a state which will allow final revision, with little additional investment, once other Centre commitments make staff time available.

Test Development (Ain Shams University Proficiency Examination)

The need was identified for a proficiency examination based on secondary school course content to measure the proficiency of students in the early stages of their university career.

Final work is in progress to complete two forms of the test, each with two alternatives. These forms have been developed through extensive trialling at Ain Shams and elsewhere. ASUPE has proved a major contribution to the evaluation of the undergraduate curriculum project, and data has been collected from a wide range of universities.

The ASUPE project has taken longer than envisaged. It has, however, produced a testing tool which can now be made available to faculties throughout Egypt to serve purposes for which no other test is currently available. This project has stimulated testing developments elsewhere, and related graduate studies and research have provided the Ministry with valuable testing expertise. Rich data regarding levels of competence is now available.

Seminars and Workshops

No specific intentions were originally expressed.

In 1981 the Centre hosted the First National Symposium on English teaching in Egypt. A Second Symposium was held in 1982.

The suitability of the Centre as a national forum is a by-product of its other activities and the investment made in it.

THE PROGRAMMES (continued)

Planning What was the original intention?	Performance What was actually achieved?	Interpretation What explains the under- and over-achievements?
	At various times the Centre has conducted seminars for local and visiting speakers at which staff from other institutions are welcome. The proceedings of some of the seminars, and especially the National Symposia, are available in published form.	Along with the graduate library, and because of its non-departmental status, the Centre has a flexibility of operation and a range of resources which makes it an excellent centre for 'catalyst' work of this kind, while its collaborative nature makes it a natural context for international contributions to professional debate.
Research and Development No specific intentions but the Centre was envisioned as a national resource rather than a simple contribution to Ain Shams programmes.	The Centre library is well used by graduate students, many of them from other universities. The stock of MA studies produced by the Centre complements those produced elsewhere, and a research register compiled by the Centre is nearing publication. Future proposals now awaiting confirmation reveal the extent to which the newer faculties and the Ministry are prepared to look to the Centre for research and development inputs into their own programmes.	This function again is essentially a product of other programmes rather than an independent objective in its own right. There exists at present no focus for professional improvement in TEFL in Egypt, though many institutions are independently doing excellent work. The ability to perform such a focusing function cannot be established overnight: it is a matter of institutional and personal reputations slowly built up and material resources gradually strengthened. Yet the ability ultimately to perform the function of servicing and initiating national professional research and collaboration is a highly significant and distinctive contribution to TEFL curriculum improvement.

Block 2—*teacher trainers*—has been the primary focus of the Professional Diploma programme. Internally, this programme has proved efficient. It would have been more effective if greater attention had been paid to questions 2.1, 2.1. 2.3 within the block; and elsewhere to questions 3.3, 3.4, 3.6; 4.1, 4.2, 4.3; 6.3, 6.5; 7.2, 7.3, 7.5; 8.2, 8.5. That is to say, problems have been encountered in terms of recruitment into, incentives for, and deployment following training rather than in the nature of the training itself.

The MA in TEFL programme can be seen as a block 3—*training programmes*—initiative in the sense that the content of the programme itself received more attention than a full analysis of implementational and recruitment considerations. Much the same set of issues arises as has been identified for the Diploma.

Block 4—*plant and equipment*—has never been the focus for Centre development, the assumption being that resources would be made available as activity required. Aid support apart, this has proved to be an unsafe assumption; that is to say, the block 4 implications (which have close connections with block 7 and block 8 matters—*funding* and *management*) have not been fully attended to, leaving issues which need to be resolved before future CDELT activity can be implemented.

A major component of CDELT activity—the curriculum development project—has been initiated through block 5—*materials*. It is interesting to note the very positive effect of this starting-point on developments in other blocks. Most significantly, the activity on question 5.3.—replacement of materials in use—has enforced question 5.6—the production of detailed teacher texts. This in turn has raised the whole set of questions regarding PERSONNEL set out in blocks 1-3. The introduction of new materials has caused both the project workers and the collaborating institutions to question existing teaching contexts (class size, criteria for grouping, course structure) and existing teacher competences (and the need for supervision and training). While it has proved possible to build some orientation into the trialling phase of the current project, the materials production activity has pointed the way to extensive future curriculum improvement through PERSONNEL factors (possibly strengthening demand for Centre assistance in this way through its graduate programmes).

The shortcomings in the materials-based (block 5) programme can be traced to essentially administrative factors. Some of the project materials produced proved inadequate and were rejected, because of the lack of experience of team members in these areas. This can be interpreted as a failure to relate questions in block 8—project *management* and the appointment and control of staff—to the intentions defined in block 5 (specifically, what sort of materials in what academic areas, replacing what?). One of the problems of project evolution is that original intentions may change—and frequently, as in the CDELT experience, expand—but project staff remain the same and have to turn their hands to tasks for which they were not originally appointed.

The major problem militating against success in the materials programme, however, has centred on disputes over *project management and responsibility*, leading to decisions to participate in and withdraw from the project which have been made on partisan rather than purely academic grounds. The establishment of a new institution — particularly one which does not fit directly into the existing 'departmental' structure — inevitably raises questions of conflicting responsibilities and areas of influence and activity: it is very easy to create antagonisms and misunderstandings which can interfere with progress. It would be dishonest to ignore this aspect of the CDELT experience. Such misunderstandings can be traced to a complex of questions in the 'spider's web': 1.1, 1.2, 1.7, 1.8; 2.1, 2.2, 2.6, 2.7, 2.8; 3.5, 3.7; 4.1, 4.5; 5.3, 5.6; 6.3, 6.7, 6.8, 6.9; 7.2, 7.3, 7.4, 7.5, 7.6, 7.7; and the whole of block 8. These are factors where existing institutional and individual interests are concerned: and any change — even if it is objectively seen as a change 'for the better' — impinges upon existing interests and activities. More projects succeed or fail, I suspect, on the basis of these essentially human factors than on any other contributing factor.

Enough has been said to exemplify the intricacy of implication which the 'spider's web' encompasses, and I shall not attempt to deal in this way with the strengths and weaknesses of every CDELT programme. In sum, however, it may be said that:

- CDELT training programmes have been academically efficient but their effectiveness has been constrained primarily by questions of incentive;
- CDELT materials programmes have been limited in one sense by questions of management and the 'human factor'; but have over-achieved in terms of outreach and in terms of the impetus generated for personnel development;
- independently motivated programmes have in the course of their development proved mutually supporting (e.g. ESP/graduate programmes; materials/testing);
- CDELT's main programmes have established the Centre as a forum for local, national and international exchange of expertise;
- while the balance of current (and envisaged) CDELT activity is different from that originally planned, the changes have been in response to local needs and realities: *what is objectively desirable is not always realistically appropriate and acceptable, and project evolution is a process of continual (and at times cladistic) adjustment to the environment of change.*

V. Planning and performance: some practical suggestions

How then can we minimize the negative effect of evolutionary change in projects and reduce the number of false starts and blind alleys while maximizing our ability to respond to the positive implications of a curriculum initiative? There are, I suggest, certain operational procedures which can help.

Taking things step by step

Too much has been written about project management procedures to make extensive recapitulation necessary here. In simple terms the planning and performance of a project requires that the following steps are followed (though a step once taken may be taken again—and again—at a later stage):

1. A problem or need is recognized.
2. The real problem or need is identified.
3. Possible solutions or fulfilment programmes are considered.
4. The implications of each are followed through (the 'spider's web').
5. A course of action is decided (the 'operational design').
6. Personnel and resources are negotiated.
7. All interested parties are involved.
8. Implementation commences.
9. Formative evaluation and regular reporting is conducted.
10. At an appropriate point, a summative evaluation is carried out and the cycle is repeated/adjusted/terminated.
11. Experience is disseminated.

Taking things slowly

Too often steps 1–7 are taken too quickly, with the result that the wrong problem may be tackled, or the wrong solution attempted, or the implications of change inadequately considered, or inadequate resources made available, or interested parties antagonized. Any of these shortcomings may sow the seed of failure or, at the least, underachievement.

Another reason for measured preparation is the need to communicate. Not only does the project team (which is often put together before completion of all these stages) need to communicate with the administrators and financial authorities upon whom the success of the project largely rests, as well as with those directly affected by the project (the teachers, the trainers, etc.). In addition, a project team needs to communicate *within* itself—to clarify the different preoccupations and preconceptions and values which individual team members hold. The CDELT experience has been a vivid example of the extent to which different national (Egyptian, American, British) perspectives —even terminologists—vary, and of the benefit which can be gained from putting together these national—and personal—views into a joint synopsis of the task ahead. Too often, a team is set to work without the time for this professional familiarization, the opportunity to identify varying interests and strengths and put them to work in the context of the programme. And failure to recognize these differences of standpoint can lead to dissension later.

Laying things open

There is a natural tendency, in embarking on a new and perhaps experimental course of action, to feel defensive — to wait until the results are available to justify the initiative. As a result, quite often those who have a legitimate interest in the effects of an innovation are given little or no control over it or even perhaps information about it. A part of the process of setting out the implications of a project (step 4) is the identification of interested parties: and a product of this should be the establishment of a forum (the working party; the steering group; the .governing body) which allows all parties to be aware of and involved in the decision taken. Sometimes, inevitably, those decisions are different from ones which the project team acting independently would have reached: but they are significant and must be heeded — they are a sign of the appropriacy of the programme, and indicate points of view which if not taken account of in the process of curriculum innovation will undoubtedly afterwards affect the success of its product.

Getting things moving

In many projects the definition of the problem and its solution is taken to be not only necessary but sufficient. Yet a curriculum project like any other endeavour requires efficient management: this requires definition of responsibilities, guarantee of resources, specification of deadlines, and the clarification of the criteria and processes for ongoing evaluation. The operational design of a project needs to be specific in these areas, and while it should be flexible in that adjustments can be made because of policy changes or practical constraints it must be drawn up at the outset and not made up as the plot of the project unfolds.

Keeping an eye on things

Given a detailed problem/solution identification, clear communications and a definite operational design, the task of assessing progress and, where necessary, adjusting ends and means become relatively straightforward. Clearly, there is little to be gained by avoiding evaluation until the end of the project at which time it may be possible to identify weaknesses but not rectify them, catalogue achievements but not expand upon them. The roles of implementer and evaluator need not conflict provided the criteria for evaluation are accurately stated: indeed, during the process of development it is probably the insider who can provide the explanatory insights which the outside assessor might lack.

Balancing inputs

Finally, it seems to me worth stressing the need to identify and exploit the contributions which can be made by different parties to the curriculum process. It is apparent that the outside expert has certain inputs to make — he may be the native speaker; he may have background experience elsewhere; in academic or professional terms he may have a distinctive contribution to make. In terms of context and process, however, the local is the expert. In watching how the web trembles, it is the host who can identify the implications and see the means by which negative effects can be avoided or at the least minimized. The value of a time for joint brainstorming at the outset of a project — for the negotiation of agreed objectives, procedures, roles, and criteria for success — cannot be over-estimated.

Conclusion

I have suggested that curriculum innovation can be initiated through primary stress on one of a number of general factors, but that whatever one's starting-point the probability is that all factors in the educational and project context will eventually come into play. I have further suggested that an advance awareness of the implications of curriculum change may assist in the avoidance of unwanted effects and the exploitation of the positive and spreading impetus that a well-directed project can create.

In all projects, and CDELT is no exception, the results differ from the expectations, in part exceeding and in part falling short of what was anticipated. *I believe that such variation is an essential and desirable part of curriculum development, created by the interaction between the innovation and the context into which it is planted.*

Curriculum development is a dynamic process, not fully predictable at the outset and dependent in large measure upon the personalities who are involved: education is about people. This truism needs to be reflected as much in our project evaluations as in our project designs. If in attempting an objective statement of project performance we may feel that we are somehow underrating ourselves and our colleagues, we need only to refer back to our spider's web with all its complexity and to Shakespeare:

> The web of our life is of a mingled yarn good and ill together: our virtues be proud if our faults whipped them not; and our crimes would despair if they were not cherished by our own virtues.

Notes

1. Specifically, I acknowledge my thanks to: Ain Shams University Faculty of Education (the host institution); United States International Communication Agency, United States Agency for International Development, Bi-national Fulbright Commission, University of California at Los Angeles (American supporting agencies); British Council, Overseas Development Administration (British supporting agencies); and to my colleagues — Egyptian, American, British — on the CDELT 'team'.

2. I have commented elsewhere on the danger of a purely anecdotal and subjective exchange of project experience. At the same time, it is easy for objective evaluation models to exclude those more human and unpredictable elements which can be critical within a project, and to fail to capture the 'illuminative' insights of the insider in the process. Reference to Lawton (1978) for the general issues here may be followed by reference in the context of ELT projects to Bowers R. G.: 'War Stories and Romances: exchanging experience in education' in ELT Docs. 'Projects in Materials Design'.

References

BOWERS, R. G., BRUDER, M. and SLAGER, W. (1980) CDELT Ain Shams: Evaluation Report, February 1980 (mimeo).
BOYDELL, T. H. (1971) *A Guide to the Identification of Training Needs.* British Association for Commercial and Industrial Education: London.
ERAUT, M., GOAD, L. and SMITH, G. (1975) The analysis of curriculum materials. University of Sussex Education Area Occasional Paper.
LAWTON, D. (1981) Curriculum evaluation: new approaches. In: LAWTON, D. *et al.*, *Theory and Practice of Curriculum Studies.* Routledge & Kegan Paul: London.
National Council for Educational Research (1981) *Education in Egypt.* Ministry of Education: Cairo.
SHAKESPEARE, W. *All's Well That Ends Well.*

Postcripts

By March 1983 the following developments were noted:

Undergraduate curriculum revision

A University Course in English for Egypt is now in use in eleven faculties of education, and is under consideration by five others (including three at the University of Ain Shams). Test evidence suggests that the materials will effect significant improvements on student standards in all four skills, with achievement at the end of year one approximating to that otherwise achieved by the middle of year three of the undergraduate course.

A new project, on a three-year time-scale, has as its aim the analysis and improvement of the curriculum in the third and fourth years. With British aid support and probable American collaboration, a working group under CDELT's Deputy Director is working closely with three other universities to a plan which envisages developments in materials, support services and training programmes.

Postgraduate training programmes

The Professional Diploma turned out fourteen well-qualified trainers/supervisors in 1981/82, has fifteen under training in 1982/83, and plans for twenty in 1983/84. Some of these trainees are engaging in in-service training activity linked to a CDELT/Ministry of Education project (see below).

Arrangements are in hand for the MA to recommence in 1983/84 with appropriate equivalence agreed. The suggestion of Summer Institutes has, however, not progressed.

ESP curriculum development

There has been no progress in this sector.

Test development

ASUPE, renamed EPEE (English Proficiency Examination for Egypt), is now provided free of charge to any faculty wishing to use it. Ten faculties currently do so. CDELT provides a data analysis services and produces an annual examiners' report. In due course alternative forms will be produced, and demand is beginning to be felt for test components which will more satisfactorily assess the extended productive skills.

Seminars and workshops

A Third National Symposium takes place in March 1983 on the theme of Teacher Education. Monthly seminars and workshops, usually with visiting speakers from US or Britain, have taken place in the current year. Closer collaboration with the Ministry of Education (see below) is involving CDELT staff in Ministry training programmes throughout the country.

Research and development

A considerably strengthened library collection is increasingly made use of by students and staff of other institutions.

In-service training

As a new initiative, planned to be pursued over a three-year period, CDELT is collaborating closely with the Ministry of Education in the production of 'training packages' for use within Ministry training programmes for the non-specialist teacher of English in preparatory schools. This materials-based programme is already having impact on matters of teacher trainers and training programmes, and interlocks closely with the other two major areas of CDELT interest – undergraduate and postgraduate studies.

CDELT administration

The last year has seen major advances in local administration and support. Both policy and day-to-day management are now the full responsibility of our Egyptian colleagues; an increasing academic and professional load is undertaken by senior and junior Egyptian staff; additional provision has been made in terms of premises, equipment, running costs. The Centre is now very much an Egyptian institution with aid support rather than vice versa. It is this indigenization which can claim the major credit for the advances which this postscript reflects.

Another major contribution to these advances has been the formulation of CDELT activity in terms of clearly defined project areas, each with a definite set of time-bound objectives.

A third element in this positive evolution has been the willingness of the aid agencies, British and American, to see curriculum innovation as a long-term process requiring long-term inputs. Extension of full-time attachments to CDELT through the KELT scheme (now a seven-man team), and the continuing support of USIS and other American agencies through specialist visits and special activity funding, has allowed the Centre to build on the activity of earlier years.

CDELT now has a clear three-year (1982–85) programme based on three key activity areas:

— pre-service teacher education through curriculum renewal in the faculties of education: change via *materials* and *personnel*;
— in-service teacher education through development of modular training packages for use by the Ministry of Education: change through *materials*, immediately affecting *training personnel* and *programmes*;

— advanced teacher education through postgraduate programmes for both Ministry trainers/supervisors and Faculty staff: change through *personnel.*

Around these three key areas, CDELT is able to maintain its other ongoing activities in research and dissemination.

Problems still exist, particularly regarding the *funding* and *management* and *plant and equipment* and *support services* implications of new patterns of activity and greater financial self-sufficiency. Undoubtedly, the progress of the Centre is still strongly influenced by 'performance factors' (including personalities) as well as by planning factors. But evolution is taking place, and is positive.

This process of positive evolution has been promoted by two growing awarenesses: first, the many-sided implications and responsibilities which the initiation of curriculum change involves; secondly, the many and wide-ranging benefits that fall from a gentle shaking of the web.

All's well that ends well.

THE INTRODUCTION OF SERVICE ENGLISH COURSES IN ESL TERTIARY INSTITUTIONS IN AFRICA

JAMES DRURY

Kenyatta University College, Nairobi, Kenya

Introduction

First of all I must say that the title is too wide — having caught your eye. In this article I shall be referring to one teacher-training university college in Kenya and specifically to the introduction of a language and study skills course to first-year undergraduates in this establishment.

With this narrowing of focus I would be wary of proceeding except that comparable personal experiences in other ESL countries and those of colleagues suggest that there may be certain patterns in the problems associated with the introduction of service English courses at this level. This hypothesis was borne out by formal and informal discussions with colleagues at the 1980 Dunford House Seminar, where we concluded, not surprisingly, that we faced a lot of common problems and that 'a problem shared is a problem halved'. This article briefly tries to air some of these problems and gives some possible solutions in the hope that their airing will stimulate more active discussion on a wider scale.

1. The setting

Kenyatta University College, a constituent college of the University of Nairobi, is the Education Faculty of the University. Currently there are 2055 undergraduates studying for a three-year BEd in various teaching subjects, 165 two-year Diploma in Education students and approximately seventy-five postgraduate students studying at different levels up to MEd. Most under-graduates take two teaching subjects and common core courses in Education on the rough basis of two-thirds teaching subjects and one-third Education during their three-year course.

The language of instruction is English throughout the college and all students arrive with a background of at least ten years' exposure to being taught in this medium in primary and secondary schools. All students have KCF 'O' level in English (basically an adaptation of the old Cambridge Overseas Certificate) and those specializing in Language/Literature teaching have at least a pass at KACE which is a 'Literature in English' examination of advanced-level standard.

First-degree graduates are qualified to teach in Kenyan secondary schools. In fact there is a big shortfall, partly caused by a high 'dropout' rate of graduates from the education system to more attractive posts in the private and government sectors. Currently the government views this 'wastage rate' quite benevolently. At postgraduate level students are aiming towards lectureships in primary or secondary teacher training colleges in the country, and perhaps more surprisingly there is still a high dropout rate even at this level. Against this seemingly ideal language background a KELT post was introduced in 1979 in the Department of Educational Communication and Technology with a wide set of objectives. However, the one which concerns us here was to help students who are having trouble communicating and studying in English. Initial research showed that students do have some language problems associated with expectations at university level, partly compounded by a superficial adequacy at the spoken level which hides these problems until they are manifested in term papers and examinations. Also as McEldowney (1976)[1] points out this level is not central to successful English-medium study anyway. In an initial survey in 1979, lecturers were asked whether their first-year undergraduates experienced language and study skills problems. The majority of respondents felt that they did and felt that particular weaknesses lay in the field of study skills, inability to follow up library and reference materials, notetaking from lectures and making notes from written sources, presentation of papers and participation in tutorials. Tests conducted on a cross-section of that year's undergraduate intake substantiated these subjective views. Tests were based on the University Pre-tests being tested by ELTS. The British Council, London, at that time and in brief they showed that undergraduate students here do experience study skill and language problems common to many ESL situations.

The reasons for these problems against a seemingly ideal ESL language background are not really the concern of this article. Suffice it to say that the Kenyan Ministry of Higher Education has recognized that language teaching and learning here is not all that it might be and of course this does not just mean for the very small percentage who go on to study in the medium at tertiary level. In the Rationale and Objectives for an In-Service Seminar on 'Language for Learning' in August 1981, the Senior Inspector of English Language wrote:

> The importance of English in the Kenyan School Curriculum cannot be gainsaid. However, there has been a widely expressed concern voiced by the public, government officials, teachers, university lecturers and others about a gradual decline in the standard of spoken and written English among our secondary school graduates. 'O' and 'A' level examiners also express this view and sample surveys at The University of Nairobi and Kenyatta University College reveal the same problem amongst first year undergraduates. All these views points to a lack of competence in the functional use of English amongst our secondary school leavers.

So the problem is recognized at school level and steps are being taken to alleviate it.

2. The course

So if the reader will accept the necessity of introducing a service English course without more substantive evidence being given here, we can get straight down to the nature of such a course and the problems experienced with its introduction, where teachers in similar situations may well see echoes of their experiences.

It was decided that ultimately a Language and Study Skills course should be given to all first-year undergraduates on an intensive basis in their first term, of two hours per week for thirteen weeks as a skills based course (Rea, 1979).[2]

The course would include (i) Reading skills with emphasis on skimming, scanning, study reading and critical reading, inference and implication, use of the library and other sources of information. (ii) Writing skills with emphasis on different types of writing skills needed at university level, the stages of writing an assignment and preparing for and writing examination answers. (iii) Reference and notemaking skills with emphasis on abstracting references and notemaking and taking from lectures and written sources, (iv) Study skills with emphasis on organization of a personal study schedule and study and memorization techniques. (v) Report writing as an optional extra for science students to demonstrate and practise various techniques for writing reports. The course was written on a unit basis, with each unit planned for one hour and was designed to be partly taught and partly self-study. The pilot model had in mind that ultimately the course may have to be offered on a self-access basis and so exercises were incorporated with this in mind. A pre- and post-test were also included for assessment purposes.

The composition of the course was based on staff and student questionnaire responses on study problem areas, personal observation and the findings of the Language and Study Skills Unit at Nairobi University, who were undertaking the design and implementation of a similar course at that time. Obviously it was also based on the patterns of published Study Skills courses available, specifically Wallace[3] and Langan[4] as there were no indications that student problems varied greatly from those for which these books were designed. For the sections on improved reading efficiency, the standard texts were incorporated.

3. The problems

Since the purpose of this article is to air the problems associated with the introduction of such a course, rather than its content, I will not dwell on the composition and time division aspects. The problems can be loosely divided as falling under student and staff levels.

Student level. Obviously this makes some sweeping generalizations but questionnaire responses and personal interviews indicated that students did not feel that they really had study-skills problems. Coming from the English learning background which I have already mentioned, there was naturally a feeling that they had quite enough tuition in the language to carry them through university. As their predecessors had obviously managed somehow, this was partly substantiated, plus the fact that examination assessment does not take into account languages, apart from on a very subjective basis on the part of individual lecturers.

So we might say that there is a motivation problem for students. Whilst a course may be incorporated into the programme of language and literature students 'disguised' as Language Usage or Communication Skills (and this is exactly what was done for the pilot project) it is not so easy to 'sell' the idea to students in other disciplines. There is also an underlying amorphous resentment of more emphasis being laid on the 'colonial language' even though it is the lingua franca of the country and quite definitely has a firm base in the education system.

Students are extremely examination oriented — and so the idea of a service course without examination marks to go towards a final degree assessment lacks kudos. This impairs the progress of a voluntary self-access course because experience here and elsewhere shows that even when students arc advised of their specific shortcomings following testing, it is the ones who need it least who actually undertake a self-access course. This is quite reasonable because of the circular nature of the problem — the students with most language and study problems take longer over their studies and therefore have less time available for 'peripheral' activities which lack compulsion. Those who have more time and ability are willing to undertake them because they present less of a challenge.

It is worth adding that the simple testing conducted before the writing of the course, and pre-test results from the pilot project, did not substantiate this self-confidence in language ability. Students did have serious problems in study techniques, speed reading and notetaking and information extraction particularly and were spending much too long unprofitably on these aspects to the detriment of other parts of their university life. After the pilot course this was freely admitted by approximately 90 per cent of respondents to a post-course questionnaire.

In the writer's experience of ESL service courses there is also initially often a subjective view of failure associated with their administration. A feeling that 'with all this English behind me I should not need coaching in even more, now that I am at university' — what might be termed a 'back to school syndrome'. Psychologically, I imagine, this feeling has some base, but linguistically it does not because many of the skills to be inculcated could valuably be taught in schools at Advanced level particularly, but in practice here they are often not (see later discussion of a new Advanced level syllabus). So there should be no stigma of failure attached to something which is essentially new. Associated with this there is also a view that service courses lack academic respect ability at a stage when students are most vulnerable to the contrasting school and tertiary level learning environments. More will be said on this with respect to staff problems.

A final quite practical student problem is that their first-year timetables are so crammed that they physically have problems in accommodating two more hours per week for the 'luxury' of a service course. This problem is common in universities but it is compounded here by the taking of subjects in three areas including education. Students in the first year have an average of twenty-four to twenty-six hours per week of class contact which is increased for science students by practicals. If one accepts that assignments are taking longer because of the problem associated with study skills then the problem is increased. Students frequently have lectures from 8 a.m. to 6 p.m. with breaks in which they are supposed to squeeze the other activities; the lack of an organized study schedule is something many do quite readily acknowledge.

4. Staff level

Naturally the problems encountered in setting up a service course of this type are not exclusive and have really only been put under these separate headings for convenience.

As mentioned earlier the initial questionnaire given to staff elicited a positive response from respondents with positive suggestions about particular language and study-skills areas which might need covering. However, despite a public relations exercise emphasizing that these were confidential and not trying to probe individual lecturing techniques, only forty-five out of a staff of 235 responded. It is this apathy or active suspicion of something new which constitutes a major problem on the staff side. This extended to members of my own department and Language Panel and even initially to the Head of Department, who whilst showing tacit interest in the introduction of such a course, was loathe to actively engage Senate, College Administration and other relevant bodies in its development. This predominant feeling contrasts I think fairly sharply with the genesis of some other ESP projects, for example The University of Malaya English for Special Purposes Project.[5] Whilst there was an underlying feeling that the quality or type of English was not adequate for tertiary-level study little tangible had been done to research possibilities of improving it, with the exception of some work being undertaken, again in difficult circumstances, by the Language and Study Skills Unit at the University of Nairobi.

Coupled with this was a jealous guarding of student time. It has already been mentioned that students are very committed in their timetable schedules and even those few Heads of Department who were actively interested in such a course found it genuinely difficult to accommodate another two hours a week and still avoid clashes, and it was felt to be low on the list of priorities for student attention. Again a lack of academic respectability plays its part here. A service course can be made to look like any other academic course being offered, but the writer feels strongly that it then loses much of its validity. The units planned and written contain a lot of practical work in timed exercises, information gathering, concept formation and so on and to offer this material by the normal lecture method would be false pedagogy and compounding the problem which the course attempts to solve. Actual staffing has also proved to be a difficult problem. If student time is stretched then of course staff time is also. Lecturers in our department have an average of twelve class contact hours per week, which is quite high for an establishment at this level. Consequently lecturers are chary of being involved in teaching another two hours per week, particularly as it is in a field in which they do not necessarily have interest or ability. The pilot scheme has been designed, written and tested by one KELT officer, a counterpart and two other lecturers. This has proved manageable as student numbers have not exceeded seventy, but when we go college-wide, teaching approximately 650 students in a normal BEd first year intake, it will be necessary to involve far more staff. For this it is planned that all the special-subject-methods lecturers attached to the Educational Communication and Technology Department will be 'dragooned' into teaching. These lecturers currently teach the educational methods courses attached to specific teaching subjects so in this way we will gain access to all the necessary students with particular subject emphasis being put on the material. This will involve course induction via an inservice seminar/workshop to all, some of whom may well not be very willing participants. Involvement of so many lecturers (up to twenty-eight) has been necessitated because it is essential that groups do not exceed twenty-five in number so that a tutorial atmosphere prevails and individual problems can be aired.[6]

5. Possible solutions

Whilst the main purpose of this paper has been to air some of the problems encountered in setting up a service English course, particularly those with general application, it would not be doing justice to the college or the writer if some of the attempted solutions were not discussed. Perhaps these will also help readers to evaluate what they would have done in similar circumstances. The first assumption is that there was, in fact, a necessity for such a course and pre-course questionnaires and assessments establish this fairly well (although there was always a sneaking feeling that muddling through could be continued adequately). This is where evaluation procedures become so important and later discussion of the pilot test will go into this more. The problems discussed have been deliberately general rather than specific and so have not touched on financing a project, administrative details, reproducing material, finding source material and so on, because each course co-ordinator must have his own procedures for this. Consequently many of the problems may be summarized as public (or rather college) relations exercises. This is a fair summary on the general level and it is most important to get as many staff members and students positively supportive as possible.

Service course directors sometimes do not fully appreciate the suspicion a service course can generate in a rarified academic environment. It has already been discussed, but it cannot be overstressed, that the innovative and remedial nature of most service courses lend themselves to suspicion. Also they are frequently innovated by expatriates in an African environment which may increase suspicion. In addition they usually do not have the examination orientation which often provides a necessary study impetus, even though they are in part tools for easing the burden of these very examinations.

In the light of these remarks it is most important that all interested parties are made fully aware of what a service course is trying to achieve, even if at the student level the pilot course has to assume some sort of disguise as was the case here. So a brief survey of the steps taken at KUC for its introduction may be appropriate.

After the initial staff–student questionnaire and personal observation, a cross-section of first-year undergraduates was tested based on the British Council tests being formulated at that time (1979), a postgraduate group were also tested as a control group. After analysis a report was written based on these results and outlining objectives, possible course design content and duration of a language and study skills course. Distribution was internal to relevant administrative and faculty board members and as an information paper to all members of staff (including those who had not responded to the first questionnaire!) It was also tabled and briefly discussed in a departmental staff meeting and in more detail with the language panel of this department (Department of Educational Communication and Technology, which was to form the base for course development). At this point the first lull set in and perhaps the lesson to be learned is that reports are good back-up material but essentially for filing and not for action.

Other extraneous factors such as student strikes and consequent closures impeded the time-scale progress of the course. However, it was face-to-face discussion with Deans and Heads of Department which got more positive responses. It was still felt though that their reactions were partly paying lip service in as far as a course would be fine as long as *they* did not have to present it to Senate for ratification *et al.* Also there was a justified feeling of proof needed of what such a course could do and, where was it anyway?

So a pilot group of language students at Diploma level was identified. The choice was not really academic but the fact that staff involved with these students were co-operative and already had a Communication Skills in English course which could be modified to become the elements of a Language and study skills course. So the course already written on a unit basis was felt to adequately cover their needs, with some modification of course material. Up to now this had been a one-man show, but now two lecturers in the Languages and Linguistics Department were involved in teaching or tutoring as we preferred to call it. A twenty-six-hour course was given concentrating on reading skills, writing skills and reference and notemaking skills. Other sections already mentioned were omitted because a lack of time precluded their inclusion (one of the reasons for running a pilot scheme). A pre- and post-test were included and a student evaluation questionnaire. The results are given in Appendix 1.

Student reactions to the course were fairly predictable. Initially they had been expecting a course in the usual 'academic mould with one-way communication and were naturally a little averse to two-way communication and actually undertaking timed exercises and so on in the classroom. However, individual study-skills profiles helped to record progress in spheres like reading-speed efficiency and this was appreciated. The tutors were not too Utopian and still the favourite question was — How would all *this* data be included in a course assessment and what would the examination at the end be like?

In fact course assessment was based on the post-test results and examination questions on the theoretical and educational implications of these skills. Nevertheless, even with these constraints, general student and staff reactions were positive and students could definitely see that improvement in these language skills had valid usage in their other university subjects. Armed with this data and a course, a further report was written (maybe they are for filing but are still the only recognized way of presenting information in this academic environment) which was directed specifically towards members of the Faculty of Education Academic Board, who would have to approve the next step towards a general course from within the faculty. This was presented at a recent board meeting, discussed and referred to their curriculum development committee. The Head of Department now fully appreciates the course and sees it as a necessary adjunct to his department once the necessary administrative and academic hurdles have been crossed. It is these which we are still working at with the first term of the 1983 academic year set as the planned date for general implementation.

In the meantime, two other useful developments have taken place. First of all the KELT counterpart has successfully completed an MEd (TEO) course at Manchester University with a dissertation subject presentation on Language and Study Skills at KUC.[7] On her return the pilot course was reviewed and with agreed modifications this is now being taught by the two tutors concerned with the course material to a new BEd I intake of Literature students. The usefulness here is partly that it can be tested on a different intake, but also to see how different tutors react and how much it can be modified to an existing course outline without losing its validity. Again there is of necessity a certain amount of initial camouflage because the course is working from a calendared one called Language Use, and really comprises a term's work within a year's course. In this respect objective evaluation will not be as easy as with the Pilot I which comprised an entity in itself.

So this has been the progress of the course so far. The message perhaps is slowly slowly wins the race or 'pole pole' as they say here in Kiswahili. It has not been the intention of this article to present anything in a negative or pessimistic light, but to air some of the problems so that solutions can be considered and others in similar situations do not feel that they are alone in encountering them. It can be a frustrating exercise introducing courses which are not immediately acceptable in the environment but ultimately it is rewarding when the target group do concretely benefit from such a course.

6. Lessons to be learned

We must conclude positively with some lessons which can be profitably learned from the particular experience related above, which is particular but by no means peculiar. Firstly, if the course is to be introduced within the terms of reference of an expatriate post, such as a KELT post, there must be a prior research phase as an analysis of the target situation and even up as far as specifications of student needs.

This research via short specialist tours is obviously not foolproof and as Wingard[8] (1971) and Chaplen[9] (1970) amongst others have pointed out, there is even lack of agreement on the skills actually needed by students pursuing university courses in a second language. However, it does clarify the situation and does make the receiving college cognizant of what such a post will hope to achieve.

This ties in with the second point that if such a course is to assume the proportions of being offered college wide, this should be recognized in terms of budgeting, staffing and timetabling. Ultimately a separate service unit should be established, whose existence is recognized within the tertiary college framework as offering service courses. As such it should not be bound by the exigencies of working to an existing syllabus or an examination timetable, but could be called upon to offer tailor-made courses where and when needs arise. These needs should be either identified by departments concerned or by the service department when it is invited to analyse students' language and study-skills problems. Whether such a unit comes under the umbrella of an existing department or is a completely separate entity is not so vital. What is more important is university recognition of its role and corresponding status with regard to budgeting and staffing and legitimate access to student time. It is felt that a service course offered by a department in the guise of one of its normal academic courses will inevitably fall between the two stools of service or true academic and will end up serving neither purpose to maximum effect.

Thirdly, as has been emphasized throughout the article, it is most important that all parties involved in a service course at staff and student level are made fully aware of what it is trying to achieve. This is not said from bitter experience, but because the writer has been aware of this fact and has tried to keep it in mind at all stages of development of the course discussed. Nevertheless, attitudes can still prevail which may surprise the uninitiated. This may well be more prevalent in the ESL rather than EFL situation, where students know that they have to reach a certain high level to undertake study through the English medium.

Finally it is useful to have more than one string to one's bow in the introduction of these skills. One of the reasons why students arrive at tertiary level with shortcomings, even with a language background such as we find in Kenya, is because of gaps in language education at secondary-school level. This has already been mentioned with respect to statements made by the Senior Inspector of English—himself a Kenyan. So if it is felt that a short course at tertiary level may not be maximally effective, it is better to get at the root cause of the problem where the catchment is so much wider and possibly more unquestioningly receptive. This is hopefully being achieved here by a new General Paper at Advanced level which will be taken by all Advanced level candidates and will include various aspects of language and study skills. This will then be a compulsory part of the curriculum for all schools with 'A' level candidates. It is said hopefully because it is only now at the stage of having been accepted into the syllabus and is now being introduced into the schools. There will of course be teething problems, but it does seem to be a step in the right direction. Even if it is argued that only a small percentage of pupils go on for further study (which is questionable at advanced level) the skills can and do have wider applications than the field of academic study. If this scheme is ultimately successful, it could make a university service course of the same type redundant, but that is what is meant by a two-pronged attack, and is quite far into the future in any case.

Notes

1. P. McEldowney, *Tests in English (Overseas). The Position after Ten Years.* Joint Matriculation Board. Manchester, 1976.
2. P. M. Rea, Study skills in English. New directions. In: *Practical Papers in English Language Education*, Vol. 2, Institute for English Language Education University of Lancaster, 1979.
3. M. J. Wallace, *Study Skills in English*, CUP, 1980.
4. J. Langan, *Reading and Study Skills*, McGraw-Hill, 1978.
5. UMESPP, *The University of Malaya English for Special Purposes Project.* ELT Documents 107. The British Council, 1980.

6. J. Drury, A report on a pilot Language and Study Skills course conducted in the Languages and Linguistics Department KUC (unpublished), 1981.
7. M. N. Muchiri, A study skills course for Kenyatta University College students in Kenya (unpublished). MEd Thesis, University of Manchester, 1981.
8. P. G. Wingard, *English for Scientists at the University of Zambia*. CILT Papers. Science and Technology in a Second Language, The British Council, 1971.
9. E. F. Chaplen, The identification of non-native speakers of English likely to under achieve in university courses through inadequate command of the language (unpublished). PhD thesis. University of Manchester, 1970.

APPENDIX I

A summary of pretest and post-test results of pilot Language and study skills course. English Language DipEd I students, April–July 1981

Student number	Section A (30 marks) pretest	post-test	Section B (30 marks) pretest	post-test	Section C (40 marks) pretest	post-test	Overall percentage % pretest	post-test	+% pretest post-test
011	1.0	13.5	15.5	13.0	15.0	13.0	31.5	39.5	+ 8.0
4004	12.5	22.0	17.5	13.5	10.0	19.0	40.0	54.5	+14.5
4017	10.5	15.5	15.5	14.0	20.0	23.0	46.0	52.5	+ 6.5
4018	1.0	19.0	14.5	14.0	6.0	23.0	21.5	56.0	+34.5
4021	1.0	11.0	3.5	4.5	9.0	12.0	13.5	27.5	+14.0
4023	13.5	17.5	18.0	10.0	22.0	28.0	53.5	55.5	+ 2.0
4029	14.0	16.5	18.5	15.0	14.0	20.0	46.5	51.5	+ 5.0
4033	11.5	16.0	16.5	13.5	9.0	19.0	37.0	48.5	+11.5
4035	22.5	17.5	21.5	11.5	16.0	20.0	60.0	49.0	−11.0
4036	6.6	10.0	9.0	13.5	13.0	26.0	30.5	49.5	+19.0
4037	15.5	16.0	19.0	15.5	23.0	20.0	57.5	51.5	− 6.0
4040	13.5	13.0	9.5	10.5	12.0	19.0	35.0	42.5	+ 7.5
4041	17.0	21.5	23.0	18.5	17.0	25.0	57.0	65.0	+ 8.0
4042	15.5	20.5	20.5	14.0	14.0	13.0	50.0	47.5	− 2.5
4043	5.5	7.5	19.0	12.0	16.0	19.0	40.5	38.5	− 2.0
4048	8.5	24.0	16.0	12.0	20.0	23.0	44.5	59.0	+14.5
4052	10.0	—	15.0	—	12.0	—	37.0	—	—
4053	7.0	18.0	17.0	14.5	16.0	18.0	40.0	50.5	+10.5
4056	—	21.5	—	14.5	12.0	18.0	12.0	54.0	—
4060	13.0	20.0	18.0	12.0	17.0	21.0	48.0	53.0	+ 5.0
4062	23.5	18.0	18.0	14.5	15.0	18.0	56.5	50.5	− 6.0
4066	10.0	17.0	16.0	18.5	23.0	23.0	49.0	58.5	+ 9.5
4068	7.0	10.0	12.5	14.5	7.5	14.0	27.0	38.5	+11.5
4069	19.0	14.5	12.5	13.5	17.0	28.0	42.5	55.5	+13.0
4070	8.0	17.0	16.0	12.0	13.0	27.0	37.0	56.0	+19.0
4077	7.0	24.0	17.0	17.0	17.0	29.0	41.0	70.0	+29.0

								Variations
4079	6.0	16.0	11.0	9.0	27.0	31.0	54.0	+ 23.0
4081	9.0	15.0	9.5	8.0	19.0	29.0	43.5	+ 14.5
4089	7.5	15.0	14.5	10.0	19.0	31.0	48.5	+ 17.5
4091	9.5	18.5	16.0	15.0	21.0	38.5	55.5	+ 17.0
4092	10.5	20.5	15.0	16.0	24.0	37.0	59.5	+ 22.5
4096	13.0	16.5	12.5	14.0	20.0	41.5	49.0	+ 7.5
4112	20.5	17.0	15.0	15.0	20.0	56.0	52.0	− 4.0
4115	15.0	25.5	16.0	10.0	24.0	37.0	65.5	+ 27.5
4131	10.0	17.0	11.0	16.0	26.0	40.0	54.0	+ 14.0
4137	5.5	16.0	10.0	18.0	15.0	39.5	41.0	+ 1.5
4142	20.0	19.5	9.5	24.0	25.0	59.5	55.5	− 4.0
4184	9.5	19.5	14.5	14.0	19.0	39.0	53.0	+ 14.0
4187	16.0	22.5	14.0	19.0	25.0	52.0	61.5	+ 9.5
4188	18.5	16.5	12.5	7.0	16.0	42.5	45.0	+ 2.5
4194	8.0	15.5	14.0	15.0	28.0	40.5	57.5	+ 17.0
4199	19.0	21.5	17.0	10.0	22.0	45.5	61.5	+ 16.0
4213	9.0	20.5	14.5	20.0	20.0	35.0	55.0	+ 20.0
4219	14.0	23.0	15.5	28.0	21.0	58.0	59.5	+ 1.5
4221	16.5	23.5	19.0	22.0	20.0	59.5	62.5	+ 3.0
Average scores	11.61	17.72	15.77	13.56	14.65	21.11	41.47	52.68	+ 11.21
Pretest post-test average		+ 6.11		− 2.21		+ 6.46			
Variations	Number of students $^{+36}_{-7}$							

WRITING READING COURSES:
THE INTERRELATIONSHIP OF THEORY AND PRACTICE

P. J. BROWN and S. B. HIRST

University of Nairobi, Kenya

Introduction

This report considers why we, in the Language and Study Skills Unit of the University of Nairobi, decided to produce our own materials, and describes how we went about this task. We are particularly interested in how and why we did — or did not — make use of the various psychological, linguistic and pedagogical theories which we had felt offered useful bases for, insights into, or justifications of what we were actually going to teach to the students.

On receiving a commission to provide a study-skills course for a particular department, our first question was: 'Should we use a published EAP/ESP course?' For various reasons we have never found it possible to do so. Many ESP textbooks are a paradox in themselves: they claim to be at once maximally specific and usefully general. The strains created by this wish to be all things to all men are invariably, but never successfully, concealed by publisher's rhetoric. The books are bought, but rarely happily used. They have, as Swales (1980) points out, 'in many respects been an educational failure', of which the ESP teacher's insistence on writing his own materials is perhaps both cause and consequence. In Nairobi we also write our own materials and the course of their evolution and evaluation is the main concern of this paper. But it is worth considering why we decided not to use published materials, although their use would have obviated the many difficulties of writing and reproducing our own courses, and would have allowed us to provide services for a much larger part of the University.

First — to judge from several recent publications — such textbooks or courses require so much major surgery to adapt them to our own needs that it is easier to produce our own materials. The first volume of one such course, for example, has an astonishing range of exercise difficulty, ranging from exercises apparently for students with a very limited knowledge of English to others suitable for native speaker undergraduates. The same volume contains examples, of the familiar syndrome: 'If you can understand the instruction You don't need to do the exercise.' The language of the rubrics is often far more complicated than that of the exercise items. Another course and its methodology are based on a particular language theory. Even if one accepts the theory, which we don't, this 'tunnel-vision' approach severely limits its value as a response to the varied and changing demands of a typical EAP/ESP teaching situation.

A second reason for our negative decision (note: we were not *unwilling*) is the negative student reaction to a 'textbook' approach. This reaction may be peculiar to this University (although it probably isn't) but it is a valid, and in our view, conclusive argument against using a published course. This negative student reaction has several causes:

(a) The student has a very clear idea of his objectives at University: he needs to pass the exams, and every course he takes must clearly help him to do this. A study-skills course for any group of students must therefore be integrated, through the materials used and the tasks set, with the subject courses the students are following. No matter what the theoretical justification for a particular course may be in terms of linguistic theory, transfer of training, etc., unless the *student* perceives its relevance and value, the study-skills course will fail. In our experience no published course satisfies this student demand in terms of relevance and authenticity, both of text and context.

(b) A single-textbook course is perceived as a school-type course. The 'textbook' at the University is not 'the course', but rather a basic source of information on to which lectures and other reading are grafted. The student naturally rejects any ESP teacher's attempt to revoke his newly acquired undergraduate status, by withdrawing physically (as he sometimes can) or psychologically (as he always can).

(c) This lack of 'face validity' of a textbook is compounded by its status as a source of information, clearly subordinate to the lecturer's tutorials, lectures, handouts and reading lists.

We do not necessarily agree with these student judgements, but they *must* be taken into account in planning any course.

The third, and most important, reason why we do not make use of published materials is that our courses necessarily have their genesis in close collaboration with members of a Department or Faculty. A reading-skills course, for example, will derive as far as possible from a week-by-week matching of our material with the current topic(s) in a departmental course or courses (cf. Appendix). In a writing-skills course, the assignment and its accompanying reading list will be drawn up in co-operation with the Department. No textbook can provide material for this level of integration.

In writing and teaching our materials therefore we must satisfy the following criteria of acceptability:

(a) the *students'* perceptions of their requirements in terms of passing examinations, and obtaining good grades;
(b) the *Departments'* perceptions of their requirements in terms of relevance, authenticity and supportiveness of material;

(c) *our* perception of (a) and (b), together with *our own* requirements in terms of theory (psychological, linguistic, pedagogical), unit and course objectives, course content and method, and unit and course evaluation.

We are here concerned chiefly with (c), our own requirements, and in particular with our attempts to make use of various theoretical insights and approaches in our writing and teaching of EAP courses in the University.

1. Theory and Practice

Every EAP practitioner in such a setting watches in his 'skul cinema' a continuous interplay of numerous theoretical positions and the promptings of varied practical experience. Theory and practice impinge on each other in varying ways and at varying depths; there is no discernible 'interface'. The link between theory and the shape of materials may be relatively direct — the materials are explicit derivations of a particular theory; or so indirect that no link is visible — yet *some* theory must inform the writing, which is clearly not composed at random.

In our own work we have observed that our initial theoretical ideas and the ultimate form of the materials are related in various ways:

(a) We may accept a theory or attempted explanation initially but find no successful pedagogical applications for it. This may lead to a modification or rejection of the theory (although not, of course, simply on pedagogical grounds) or we may continue to regard it as a plausible hypothesis without present application.
For example: the concept of 'prediction' in reading, put forward (among many others) by Goodman (1967) and Smith (1978).

(b) We are not sure of the validity of a theory, i.e. whether it explains what it purports to explain, but we continue to base materials on it because it is pedagogically fruitful and it 'works'.
For example: reading as an omnibus skill consisting of a number of sub-skills.

(c) We do not accept existing theory, or there are so many competing and conflicting theories to explain the same phenomenon that our materials must be built on the purely practical foundations of needs analysis, experience, trial and error, etc.
For example: explanations of what makes a 'good reader' and distinguishes him from a 'bad reader'.

(d) Although no theory known to us is entirely satisfactory, we often find a suggestion, a definition or an insight by a writer illuminating and fruitful for materials writing.

For example: we could find no satisfactory theory of comprehension (cf Bormuth; Carroll; Frederiksen, 1972),[1] but we did find Scriven's description of comprehension as 'a function of contextual demands' (Scriven, 1972) a most helpful starting-point in considering our particular problems.

(e) In some areas, a great deal of research has yet produced no theory which provides any adequate starting point for the writing of materials.
For example: discourse analysis.

The remainder of this paper will consider in more detail the interaction of theory and practice as we have experienced it in writing and teaching. We shall deal with some areas which concern the writer of EAP materials: reading, comprehension and evaluation.

2. Reading

A consideration of the problems encountered by students in their reading logically begins with an examination of the activity of reading itself. Here is the text, a cat's cradle of medium and message, language and content, overlapping and interrelated in ways still imperfectly understood; and here is the reader, his cognitive world waiting to be modified on confrontation with the text. Just how this modification is achieved, we do not yet know: there are a number of competing hypotheses. We should like therefore briefly to consider two widely held views of the reading act and describe our experiences in adopting them as a framwork for materials writing.

(a) Writers such as Goodman (1967) and Smith (1978) suggest that an important aspect of successful reading is a reader's ability to use linguistic and non-linguistic information to make predictions or form hypotheses about what is coming next — 'next' being variously defined as sentence, paragraph, or chapter. If, as Smith argues, a readiness to make guesses, or, as Goodman puts it, a willingness to take part in the 'psycholinguistic guessing game' is a characteristic of a good reader, then exercises to develop the techniques of prediction would be a vulnerable addition to our range of teaching materials. However, we have found it extremely difficult to devise such materials and even more difficult to confirm that they were of any value to our students. The only recent materials specifically designed for the same purpose that we have seen (*Skills for Learning*, 1980 and 1981) do not seem to us to involve prediction techniques so much as valid/invalid inference.

One reason for our difficulty is possibly that prediction is not one of the skills our students do make use of. Does any reader in fact make use of it, when faced — which is the University student's position — with a new and difficult text on an unfamiliar topic? The extent of prediction of content is chiefly a function of familiarity with the topic. And how far certain linguistic and rhetorical structures serve effectively as predictors of content (cf. Tadros, 1978) is still a matter of controversy. It seems to us that our students are far too busy trying to make sense of what they have just read and to link the sentence they are reading now to previous sentences, to have any spare processing capacity available for prediction. Their activity is chiefly retrospective, attempting to make sense of already partly processed materials, rather than forward-looking or predictive.

Furthermore, beyond the level of the sentence, the whole concept of prediction becomes notoriously more difficult to define in terms that would make sensible exercises possible. Where 'prediction' at this level has been used as a basis for practice material, there seem always to be enough defensible variant 'solutions' to make nonsense of the writer's choice of a single 'answer'. It seems to us that such attempts founder on the assumption that the linguist's *description* of the rhetorical and functional structure of a text is necessarily mirrored by the reader's method of *processing* its information, that the description of the encoded text can have psychological reality as a representation of the decoder's activities, and further, that such representations can directly determine the shape of classroom exercises.

We are all familiar with the dire pedagogical effects of a similar assumption about the psychological reality of the formal descriptions in generative grammar.

(b) A second hypothesis about the skill of reading which we have taken account of is that it is an omnibus skill comprising a number of discrete sub-skills, which can be differentiated and described and therefore perhaps taught and tested. Both our own experience and other studies suggest that this is, at the most, a very simplified version of 'reading', and possibly totally mistaken. Research by Davis (1968) and Lunzer and Gardner (1979) seems to cast doubt on the whole 'reading skills' theory. Lunzer and Gardner conclude, for example, after exhaustive statistical analysis of a wide range of research data, that 'individual differences in reading comprehension should not be thought of in terms of a multiplicity of specialized aptitudes. To all intents and purposes such differences reflect only one general aptitude: this being the pupil's ability and willingness to *reflect* on whatever he is reading' (p. 64).[2] We thus have a 'discrete skills' approach, which sees reading as the summation of micro-skills which can be taught and tested, and a 'holistic' integrated approach, which sees reading as an interaction between reader and text which cannot be usefully analysed into 'X' number of skills without totally distorting what actually goes on in the reading act.

Although we sympathize with the 'holistic' view we shall continue producing materials based on the 'discrete skills' approach, because by doing this we gain a *pedagogical* advantage in terms of the organization of materials and the writing of manageable exercises. The approach also seems to have 'face validity' in terms of student acceptance. And finally it seems to 'work'. We suspect it works because it enables us to engage the student's attention and focus his concentration on the act of reading — for whatever purpose — and it is this 'engagement', however achieved, which seems to be the vital element in reading progress.

3. Comprehension

The many hypotheses about the nature of the act of reading, of what the reader actually does in the process of 'interacting' with the text and the skills he employs to attain his objective of 'comprehension', are paralleled by equally numerous attempts to establish precisely what has taken place when a reader has comprehended a text and to distinguish possible causes of 'failure' to do so. Urquhart (1978) who describes and criticizes attempts by Bormuth and Carroll to produce an acceptable definition of comprehension, himself suggests a description of comprehension as a 'provisional construct' and concludes: 'If this involves accepting "different" comprehensions (which it does), then we will just have to be flexible about this' (Urquhart, *op. cit.*, p. 45). This conclusion has much in common with Scriven's description of comprehension as 'a function of contextual demands' (Scriven, 1972).

In the absence of any generally accepted definition or description of 'comprehension', and once again searching for practical teaching solutions to evident problems, we started at the other end. If we all agree that readers vary in their reading capacities, then we can ask, why do some readers find successful reading manifestly more difficult than others?

There seem to be several sources of potential difficulty, some originating in the reader, others in the text. With some of these difficulties we can help, with others we cannot.

1.   Difficulties originating in the reader

(a) The reader has *an inadequate knowledge of the signalling system* used to convey information in a particular language. Note that knowledge which is adequate at one stage, e.g. in sixth-form studies with a small number of texts and relatively intensive teacher support, may be inadequate at another stage, e.g. in first-year undergraduate studies where the above conditions do not apply. Ideally, individual diagnostic tests will indicate specific areas of weakness for each student, which can then be strengthened; in practice, of course, 'weak' readers of this kind are taught as a fairly homogeneous group.

(b) *Slow reading.* We define this as a weakness independent of the purpose of reading. It occurs when a reader processes the information so slowly that he cannot hold sufficient detail in his short-term memory to enable him to decode the overall message of the text. This weakness may derive from (a) above but in our experience is frequently displayed by readers with a more than adequate knowledge of the language system. In this case it is probably the result of reading habits learned at school where the relatively few texts are read with minute care and immense slowness. In such circumstances there is no doubt that reading speeds can be increased by suitable exercises in the tradition established by Fry (1963).

(c) *Inability to distinguish rhetorical functions* and how these may be linked. By this, we do not mean, of course, the inability to label an example, or define it, but the capacity to understand the differences between the contributions to *discourse meaning* of, for example, hypothesis and evidence, or concept and explanatory analogy, or the cohesive functions performed by sentence connectors and synonymy, hyponymy and antonymy.

(In an initial attempt to improve this weakness we first *named* a function, *defined* it, *exemplified* it and then invited students to *identify* occurrences in a text—thus falling into the familiar trap of teaching *about* language and making the whole business puzzling and irrelevant to our students. We are still working on an alternative approach, based essentially on dealing with key functions as and when they appear in our texts.)

(d) *The reader's attitude*: a frequently crippling source of difficulty is the student's lack of interest in the subject. This may be causal or consequential. In the first case the student lacks interest in the subject because he does not want to do it. He may have been forced into it because his preferred options were not available; he may dislike the lecturer, etc. His original attitude *causes* the difficulty. In the second case the student may be interested at first but for various reasons, e.g. the course moves too fast, there is more reading than he can cope with, etc., he loses his interest. His loss of interest is a *result* of his experience of the discipline. We may be able to help with the second problem; the first is not within our scope.

2. Difficulties originating in the text

(a) *Texts can be badly written*, both in an absolute and a relative sense. In the absolute sense the writer is so involved in his 'intolerable wrestle with words', his struggle to express his thoughts to himself that he is never able to stand back from what he has written and view it, in some sense, as a future reader —he is only addressing himself. We do not know of any way in which we can prepare a reader to cope specifically with this kind of text.

In a relative sense a text may be badly written in that the information load may be too great even for the audience for which it was designed. This weakness is especially common in scientific texts; it seems to be assumed that any kind of redundancy is a sign of bad writing, even in introductory texts for first-year students. Information is inefficiently communicated and is only netted by the student, if at all, after numerous readings—which seems to be the only solution to the problem.

(b) *Texts may be unsuitable* for a particular student or group. The writer's expectations of what his reader will bring to the text in terms of previous reading, knowledge of the subject, degree of experience, etc., are not fulfilled. Either the student is voluntarily reading a more specialized text than he is ready for or his department has made an inappropriate selection. The solution to these problems is not within our province.

We have, then, indicated six possible sources of reading difficulty:

1. From the student himself:
   (a) He does not know the linguistic system well enough.
   (b) He reads too slowly.
   (c) He cannot decode the rhetorical structure.
   (d) He lacks motivation.
2. From the text:
   (a) Bad writing, either obscure or overloaded.
   (b) Text unsuitable for certain readers.

Since we are unlikely to be able to change the texts which a department or faculty selects, although we may offer advice, we can only attempt to deal with the first three sources of difficulty, and thereby hope to remedy the fourth. By thus distinguishing between those problems we can help to solve and those we can't, we can provide the basis for a pragmatic solution to our materials-writing problems, even in the absence of a satisfactory definition of comprehension.

4. Evaluation

We are involved in testing and evaluation in three areas:

1. The testing of first-year students by means of criterion-referenced reading and writing tests designed to identify potentially weak students and diagnose their weaknesses.
2. Pre- and post-testing of courses written by members of the Unit; the testing is done in terms of the *objectives of the course.*
3. Evaluation of the work of the Unit in terms of its effect on *student performance in their own subject areas.*

1.   Testing of first-year students

The Language and Study Skills Unit was originally set up in response to a general anxiety of the University authorities about the adequacy of student performance. This was expressed in such terms as 'They don't seem to do any reading', or 'They can't write an essay'. Our first task was to construct a battery of tests to discover whether Faculty unease was justified and to provide objective evidence on which to base course proposals. Our tests were criterion-referenced and (with the consultancy help of Brendan Carroll) modelled on versions of the current tests of the Council's English Language

Testing Service. More than 2000 students have now taken these tests, but there are certain aspects of them which we now feel are not satisfactory.

(a) The tests have been written with the aid of a (Munby-esque) inventory of the skills to be tested, but they are far from being structuralist discrete-point tests; they include discourse-level questions and questions on text-graphic relationships. However, they appear to be insufficiently pragmatic: 'They do not require sufficient attention to meaning in temporally constrained sequences of linguistic elements'.[3] Even note-making or summarizing questions, with an *ulterior* purpose, which would seem to qualify as pragmatic tests in this sense, can be coped with in a mechanical and uncomprehending manner: a student can produce even an acceptable summary without understanding. Here we return to Scriven's (*op. cit.*) relativist definition of comprehension as a 'function of contextual demands'. Each task facing the student calls for a different level of 'comprehension': joining in a discussion, passing an examination, completing an otherwise meaningless exercise with the minimum effort required to avoid trouble with the tutor – all these make different demands on the student and the tester. And reflecting on our now much greater experience of how a student actually copes with his academic work here, it seems to us that we do not yet take enough account of the Nairobi University extra-linguistic context in devising our test items.

(b) A second source of misgiving about our tests is that there is a lower correlation between reading and writing results than we expected and than, in the original design, we assumed there would be. In this year's Arts Faculty tests, for example, of the 133 students who scored less than 50 per cent in the reading skills section, only thirty-nine were graded as unsatisfactory on the writing test, on the basis of grades given by three independent markers. In other words, many who did badly on the reading test wrote quite acceptable essays. Similar results have occurred in earlier years.

The explanation may be that although the essay questions were accompanied by reference texts for use in the preparation and writing of the essay, a student with a good general knowledge of, say, *The Population Problems of the Third World* could write an acceptable essay without having read the supporting texts. But how did he acquire this knowledge except by wide reading? And yet the reading test identified him as a poor reader.

2.   Pre- and post-testing of courses

Our main problem here is probably common to all ESP projects without an institutionalized research element. Evaluation of a course requires first a pre-test of two groups of students – those taking the course and a control group not taking it. The two groups need to be matched, not only, as is usual, in terms of the range of linguistic skills, but also in terms of 'context' – the University courses which the students are taking, and the students' initial knowledge, if any, of the subject discipline. The post-test, which should really be a subject test devised by the subject lecturer, ought to reveal that the group subjected to the study-skills course has performed better. Even if such results have been obtained elsewhere, it is no doubt often assumed that they are due to the course, but such assumptions can never be adequately tested in the presence of many other variables. In Nairobi we have not yet been able to set up control groups. Departments in which we have worked have so far always refused to allow any of their students to be 'left out' of a study-skills course.

If a post-test is given in the form of an identical or 'matched' study-skills test, rather than a subject test, results which indicate an improvement in 'reading skills' may simply be characteristic of the whole University population. At the linguistic level we have in Nairobi, mere attendance at the University must surely do something to improve students' reading ability. On the other hand, results which indicate deterioration may be due to student attitudes towards a study-skills post-test, especially if this is an identical rather than a 'matched' test: they will be irritated at having to take for the second time a test which is manifestly not part of a degree course. We should be interested to known whether other projects *working at a similar linguistic level* have been able to handle this problem of course evaluation and validation in an unchallengeably rigorous way.

3. Students' performance in their own subject areas

The final purpose of our courses is that students perform better in their subject disciplines, that, for example, at the end of a reading-skills course for Land Development students, they should be able to read their professional texts faster and more effectively than they were able to before the course. Post-tests on the study-skills course itself (see above) can only tell us at the best whether the students have 'learnt' what we have taught them. This is not the same as showing that (a) what we have taught them is in fact useful in their subject disciplines or that (b) even if it is, the students do in fact use their newly acquired skills in the target context, i.e. that there is any transfer of training. Comparisons, for example, between the end of year results of different years in the same department, e.g. between the class of '80' who have not taken course X and the class of '81' who have (in the absence of comparable groups within the same year) are stultified, as we have noted above, by contaminating variables such as different lecturers, different recommended textbooks, even a different grading policy introduced by a department or lecturer. At a different linguistic level, for example at the English Language Centre, KAAU, Jeddah, objective criteria for evaluation are available in terms of task performance, thus providing operational definitions of objectives. But in a context where almost all students are *linguistically* competent, and the ideal study skills component we are working towards is one that ceases to have any existence independent of the subject discipline (and indeed may not be taught by members of the Unit, see

Appendix) then it is difficult to see how the contribution of that component to a student's success can be separately identified or evaluated.

In the absence of acceptable objective criteria for study-skills-promoted improvement in a specific discipline we have three alternative sources of validation:

(a) The first is our own judgement of the effectiveness of a course. Training and experience enable us to make judgements which at least deserve to be seriously considered.

(b) The second source of validation is the opinion of the students. Each of the Unit's courses is followed by a questionnaire on specific aspects of the course, such as administration, pace and timing, content, methodology and transfer of training. Past responses to these questionnaires have dictated many features of our courses.

(c) The third source of validation is those departmental members of staff responsible for teaching first-year students. They are always consulted at each stage of the writing process; they often observe the study-skills classes. After the completion of the course they are also asked informally to give their assessment of the effects of the course on the work of the students in their specific subject.

5. Conclusion

In this paper we have set out to examine the interaction between certain theories, our attitudes to them, and our application of them in the production of reading-skills courses in particular. We can offer no algorithms, no charts to guide other writers, for we have found each writing and teaching situation unique, and defined by a unique set of variables, such as existing theory, the level of departmental co-operation, subject characteristics and student attitudes. Many of our decisions and procedures have been based on intuition, in its turn based on, we hope, relevant experience: 'This will, or will not, work.' Not surprisingly, we have found some insightful theoretical approaches unusable and some dubious ones pedagogically valuable. We are least happy about the area of evaluation, so plainly essential in theory, so clear in conception, and yet, in our particular context, so unsatisfactory, so unclear and so unrigorous in practice. We agree with the comments of a participant at Dunford House: 'More research and more production needs to be done in this area, and the question of whether ESP *requires special types of testing and evaluation* needs to be tackled' (Dunford House, 1978).

If, for example, our course objectives could be defined in terms of the students' successful performance of tasks *within the discipline* (tasks which they could not perform *at all* before the course), then the evaluation of such performance is clearly the province of the subject lecturer and not of the Unit. Moreover, as we have observed (see Section 5), the extent of the contribution of a student's linguistic and study-skill competence to his successful performance of the task remain unknown.

We cannot pretend that our development has been marked by the uniformly satisfactory and successful application of theoretical insights in a logical and coherent manner resulting in the production of materials and courses which manifestly achieved clearly defined objectives. Since many ESP 'war stories' are suspiciously neat, like the autobiographies of generals who were sacked, we have, we hope, been frank and untidily pragmatic enough to be both credible and useful. We have been struck by the extraordinary difficulty of utilizing our theoretical knowledge in a thoroughgoing way, and the frequent necessity of reviewing our whole approach towards any particular course. Our most successful approaches have been characterized by flexibility — but this does not make for neatness, coherence or ease of evaluation. We are learning all the time about what will or will not work, what is or is not acceptable. We live in an atmosphere of (we think) creative uncertainty, we are constantly involved in arguments, which we prefer to describe as discussions, about theory, methodology, evaluation; we are inordinately pleased by approaches which 'go well', and correspondingly depressed by the failure of apparently sure-fire approaches. Perhaps most EAP projects at a similar level exist in such an atmosphere.

Finally we append a brief description of a (mark 2) course for the Department of Sociology which we are in the middle of writing and teaching. This illustrates the point that each course has unique characteristics which in many ways control the content, the presentation and the methodology. In this case the most unusual feature is that most of the teaching is done by the sociology tutors, themselves using our materials, the eventual aim being a course totally taught by the Department with only a watching and revising brief held by the Language and Study Skills Unit. This is in accordance with our earlier expressed belief that the most desirable EAP project is the one that ceases to exist independently of the Departments and Faculties it serves.

Appendix

Title:

A reading skills course for first-year students in the department of Sociology.

Conditions:

(a) The course will be given in the tutorial hours allocated to the Department of Sociology in the Arts Faculty timetable.
(b) *All* first-year sociology students will take the course.
(c) The 177 students are divided into nine tutorial groups, each group having its tutorial hour at a different time of the week.
(d) Partly because the Unit is too small to teach all nine groups, partly because the Department of Sociology wishes to be involved in actually

teaching the course, most of the groups are taught by Sociology tutors.

(e) The students attend two formal Sociology lectures a week. The materials for the reading classes are usually drawn from the recommended reading in the basic next (N. J. Smelser, *Sociology, An Introduction*, Wiley, 1973) for that week. Thus the main topic of the weekly lectures and the content of the materials used in the reading classes are closely related.

Comments:

(a) *Reading*: most of the problems referred to in Section 3 (Reading) have been met viz.:
    (i) Parts of the text are badly written.
    (ii) Parts of the text are too advanced for the target group (the book is an anthology by various authors on different aspects of sociology).
    (iii) The book is 796 pages long. We know a number of our students will never finish it, with reading speeds as low as 95 words per minute.
    (iv) Some students find great difficulty in distinguishing rhetorical functions. They have particular problems with analogy, increased by the tendency in sociological writing for analogies to become pseudo-explanations, e.g. society as an organism, society as a watch, etc.
    (v) Student attitudes vary from those expressing great interest in and enthusiasm for the subject to those indicating the student would rather be elsewhere (he originally applied perhaps for another Faculty).

(b) *Objectives*:
Priorities for selection of materials and methods included:

    (i) *Reading speed.* We have moved away from a Fry or SRA approach where 'speed' seems an artificial and pointless imposition, to one where we regularly remind students through exercises that time is a valuable commodity, and that conscious attention to how long they take to read a text can improve both the speed at which they read and how well they will understand it; we also stress that complete understanding of everything they read is unnecessary and a waste of time. 'Understand only as much as you need to' is an alarming idea to many of our students but absolutely essential if they are to cope with the numerous reading demands made on them.

    (ii) *The rhetorical organization of sociology texts.* These texts are characterized by the regular use of certain patterns of organization, e.g. generalization followed by exemplification, or vice versa; hypothesis followed by evidence; explanation through analogy (see (a) (iv) above). Of course the students do not need to *name* these patterns, but merely to understand their contribution to the discourse meaning.

(iii) *Work in checking comprehension of the text.* We have used various note-making techniques for this, from summary gap-filling, diagram completion, etc., to complete summaries matched against a model. The tasks for this purpose must be as pragmatic as possible and therefore should not be ends in themselves.

(c) *Methodology*:

In an earlier course for the same department, our first challenge was to find a method of presentation of the material which could be handled by tutors who were not experienced in 'group-work' techniques or in demanding a high level of participation from the students; they were happier to 'stand and deliver' a set-piece lecture.

Our first attempt to deal with this problem involved writing out the materials with detailed step-by-step instructions for teacher activity, an attempt, in fact, to produce 'teacher-proof' materials. These were not successful. Either the teachers did not put in the necessary preparation time or the classes were painfully slow and boring as the tutor faithfully went step by leaden step through the material.

In the present course we are now producing more student-orientated and self-access material in the form of a weekly unit which the tutor works through with his class. The materials included in any particular unit are drawn from the reading prescribed for that week by the Sociology Department. The text is therefore authentic (although not of course in the context of presentation in a Reading-skills course, of Dudley Evans and Johns, 1981) and relevant; the exercises are sociologically useful: their end product is greater understanding of the sociological theories and concepts in the syllabus.

The members of the Unit teach the first two reading classes and are observed by the sociology tutors, the tutors then teach the other groups, and each is observed at least once by a member of the Unit. Since the sociology tutors both observe and teach the material they are able to judge its effectiveness; they are themselves guarantors of its relevance.

We are thus team-teaching. As the ultimate aim is that the materials will be taught only by sociology tutors, the test of successful materials is not how well *we* teach them, but how well *they* do. We were obliged to jettison a number of approaches which might be successful in the hands of an experienced EFL teacher, involving, for example, clearly differentiated sections *within* a lesson and requiring therefore the ability accurately to judge time spent on each section. Alternative methodologies have to be found. The tutors' constant tendency to move back into *lecturing* must be watched; and the *amount* of material that can be dealt with successfully is more limited. But the aim of the programme is logical enough: the teaching of sociology (or whatever) by sociologists with an awareness of the language problems of their students, and the materials and methodology to help solve those problems. Expressed in more general terms, this represents perhaps the ultimate ideal for many ESP/EAP projects.

Notes

1. See Urquhart's summary of the main points of these writers' theories of comprehension in Urquhart (1978).
2. Support for this unitary view can also be found in Horst Lofgren's The measurement of language proficiency, in *Studia Psychologia et Pedagogica*, Series Altera 57, WK Glierup Berlingska Boktryckerict (Lund, Sweden, 1972), quoted in Oller, p. 62 (1979).
3. J. W. Oller, *Language Tests at School.* Longman, 1979, p. 39.

References

Assessment. Handbook of the English Language Centre, King Abdulaziz University, Jeddah.
BLEICH, D. (1975) The subjective character of critical interpretation. *College English*, Vol. 36, No. 7.
CLARK, M. A. and SILBERSTEIN, S. (1977) Towards a realisation of psycholinguistic principles in an ESL reading class. *Language Learning*, Vol. 27, No. 1, pp. 135–154.
DAVIS, F. B. (1968) *Research in comprehension in reading. Reading Research Quarterly*, Vol. 3, pp. 499–545.
Dunford House Seminar Report. (1978) The British Council.
DUDLEY-EVANS, A. and JOHNS, T. F. (1981) *A Team-teaching Approach to Lecture Comprehension for Overseas Students.* ELT Documents, p. 36. The British Council, 1981.
ESKEY, E. D. A model programme for teaching reading to advanced students of English as a foreign language. *Language Learning*, Vol. 23, No. 2, pp. 169–184.
FREDERIKSEN, C. H. (1972) Effects of task-induced cognitive operations on comprehension and memory processes. In Freedle and Carroll (eds.).
FREEDLE, R. Q. and CARROLL, J. B. (1972) *Language Comprehension and the Acquisition of Knowledge.* Winston & Sons.
FRY, F. (1963) *Teaching Faster Reading.* Cambridge.
GOODMAN, K. (1967) Reading: a psycholinguistic guessing game. *Journal of the Reading Specialist*, pp. 259–264, pp. 266–271.
Language in Education (1972) The Open University. Routledge & Kegan Paul.
LOFGREN, H. (1972) The measurement of language proficiency, In: *Studia pschologica et pedagogica*, Series altera 57, Lund, Sweden.
LUNZER, E. and GARDNER, K. (1979) *The Effective Use of Reading.* The Schools Council, Heinemann Educational Books.
OLLER, J. W. (1979) *Language Tests at School.* Longman.
ROBINSON, P. (1980) *E.S.P. (English for Special Purposes).* Pergamon.
ROWNTREE, D. (1974) *Educational Technology in Curriculum Development. Harper & Row.*
SCRIVEN, M. (1972) *The Concept of Comprehension: from semantics to software.* In Carroll and Freedle (eds.)
Skills for Learning 1980, 1981 and forthcoming. Nelson University of Malaya Press.

SMITH, F. (1973) *Psycholinguistics and Reading*. Holt, Rinehart & Winston.
SMITH, F. (1978) *Understanding Reading*, 2nd ed. Holt, Rinehart & Winston.
STREVENS, P. (1977) *New Orientations in the Teaching of English*. O.U.P.
SWALES, J. (1980) E.S.P.: The text book problem. *The E.S.P. Journal*, Vol. No. 1, Fall, 1980.
TADROS, A. (1978) The notion of predictive structure and its pedagogical applications. *MALS Journal*, Summer 1978.
URQUHART, A. H. (1978) Comprehension: the discourse analysis view: meaning in discourse. In: *The Teaching of Comprehension*, ELT Documents. The British Council.

UNIQUE AND RECURRENT ELEMENTS IN SYLLABUSES FOR ESP

LEO O'KEEFFE

Department of Technical Education and Vocational Training, Zambia

Introduction

This article summarizes what we have learned while designing syllabuses in ESP for a wide range of technical and vocational subjects. Information of purely local concern has been omitted and we present extracts from a syllabus and a summary of our insights which we hope will be of use to those teaching pre-experience technical and vocational courses in a second language situation. These insights have come from designing syllabuses for future workers in the following occupational categories.

Technical and related workers:
    automotive, civil, electrical, electronic, mechanical, chemical, metal-lurgical and mining technicians
Production and related workers:
    tailors, shoemakers, woodworkers, machine-tool operators, machinery fitters, motor vehicle and aircraft mechanics, electrical and electronics fitters, radio and television repairmen, plumbers, welders, sheet-metal workers, printers, painters, bricklayers and carpenters
Clerical and related workers:
    stenographers, typists, book-keepers, cashiers
Service workers:
    hotel managers, housekeepers, cooks and waiters.

These categories are based on the classification of the International Labour Office, ILO (1969).

Studying the language needs of such a wide range of occupations gave us our major insight into the problems of multiple syllabus design. We had been prepared to write a unique syllabus for each occupation but we found that we did not have to: though different occupations need specific syllabuses, these syllabuses are rarely, if ever, unique. The technical words will differ from subject to subject but the language skills and functions, and the events and activities for which these language skills and functions are used, are usually common to a large group of occupations. Specificity does not necessitate uniqueness.

1. A sample

A good language syllabus is an expression of the educational philosophy of the writer and a summary of what is best in current trends in language teaching. It provides a support for the teacher and a guide for the student. It provides a basis for textbook selection, or, where no suitable books are available or obtainable, a basis for materials, production. A syllabus is needed for examinations, for revision and for research. It is a basis for in-service training and for discussion and negotiation within the administration. Without a good syllabus there is nothing.

The syllabus from which the following extracts are taken would normally be read with an accompanying guide to explain the difficult words and to give examples of language realizations. In use, it is preceded by a study skills syllabus which is common to all courses but which is not reproduced here. The extract given below is from a Language of Work syllabus for the industrial, or process, engineering technician. It draws heavily on Munby (1978) and on Wilkins (1976) and also makes use of Williams (1973) quoted in Candlin, Kirkwood and Moore (1975). The job description of the industrial engineering technician is adapted from the description in ILO (1969).

The syllabus starts with a brief profile of the communicative needs of the technician, outlining the purpose for which he will need English and describing his work in some detail:

> The graduate requires English as one of the national languages of Zambia. It is the language of science, technology and administration and may be used between the graduate and workers and members of the public where there is no indigenous Zambian language in common.
>
> The central duty of the graduate is the performing of technical tasks contributing to the development of processes and the installation, maintenance and repair of processing plant and equipment. The graduate

(a) sets up and carries out experiments, makes tests, takes readings, performs calculations, adjusts instruments, records observations and otherwise assists in research to develop or improve processes and manufacturing;
(b) prepares detailed estimates of quantities and costs of materials and labour required for construction and installation of plant and prepares work schedules;
(c) inspects and regulates functioning plant and equipment;
(d) exercises technical supervision and control of processing operations;
(e) gives technical guidance to workers engaged in construction, installing, maintaining and repairing plant and equipment;

(f) inspects and tests completed work to ensure compliance with specifications and safety standards;

(g) applies knowledge of processing engineering theory and practice to recognize and solve problems arising during day-to-day operations.

The profile then describes, briefly, the setting in which English is used, the people with whom English is used and the forms of English required. It sets targets for the various language skills, emphasizing that, in all industrial practice involving the safety of workers, accuracy in languages is essential.

The syllabus then lists five events which we have decided are the main language events in the work of the industrial engineering technician:

Performing technical tasks in industrial engineering.
Working with colleagues, supervisors and subordinates.
Dealing with the general public.
Contributing to the smooth running of the unit.
Maintaining and developing personal technical standards.

These events form the five units of the syllabus. Each is divided into activities and each activity is then assigned appropriate language functions. The first two units of the syllabus are given below.

Unit One: Performing Technical Tasks in Industrial Engineering

Element 01: Performing tests and experiments
    1.1 Outlining test procedures necessary for obtaining required results through
        hypothesis
        presupposition
        explanation
        clarification
    1.2 Recording observations and conclusions through
        identification involving taxonomy, matching, differentiating
        analysing involving evaluating, measuring, generalizing
        describing involving evidence, inference, quantification, explanation
    1.3 Reporting results through
        explanation
        analysis
        evidence
Element 02: Estimating quantities and costs
    2.1 Identifying equipment and materials needed through
        description
        classification
        quantification

    2.2 Identifying labour required through
         assessing, estimating
    2.3 Completing estimates by
         outlining work to be done through
            description, classification, quantification
         listing equipment or materials needed through
            identification, classification, quantification
         indicating labour required through
            rational exposition

Element 04: Giving technical guidance
    4.1 Outlining procedures to be followed using
         description
         direction
    4.2 Supervising work in progress through
         suggestion, recommendation
         advice
         instruction, direction
    4.3 Inspecting of work in progress through
         assessment
         approval
         disapproval

Element 05: Testing and inspecting completed work
    5.1 Assessing completed work through
         identification involving defining, questioning
         analysing involving evaluating, measuring
         concluding
    5.2 Making observations through
         rational enquiry
         evaluation
         approval
         disapproval

Unit Two: Working with Colleagues, Supervisors and Subordinates

Element 01: Joint consideration of problems
    1.1 Identification of problem by
         rational enquiry
         exposition
    1.2 Analysing problem by
         evaluating
         concluding
    1.3 Reaching a solution through
         argument
         agreement
         disagreement

concession
approval

Element 02: Communicating results and decisions
    2.1 Rational exposition involving
        explanation
        analysis
        evidence

Element 03: Giving instructions
    3.1 Identification of problem involving
        explanation
        analysis
        evidence
    3.2 Outlining proposed solutions through
        explanation
        justification
    3.3 Giving instructions involving
        means
        method

Element 04: Receiving instructions
    4.1 Seeking clarification by indicating
        area of doubt
        misunderstanding
    4.2 Proposing other solutions through
        rational exposition
    4.3 Accepting direct instructions by
        indicating understanding
        agreement

Element 05: Seeking permission
    5.1 Stating problem through
        explanation
        substantiation
        justification
    5.2 Making the request using conventional forms

Element 06: Granting or refusing permission
    6.1 Acknowledging request using conventional forms
    6.2 Analysing the request through
        evaluating
        concluding
    6.3 Granting or refusing permission through
        explanation
        substantiation
        justification

The three subsequent units are developed in the same way. Unit Three deals with the language of handling groups of people and handling individual general inquiries. Unit Four concentrates on aspects of official correspondence including letter writing and form filling and also deals with the language necessary for organizing or participating in formal meetings. The last unit, Unit Five, is concerned with the maintenance and development of the worker's technical standards after entering the world of work and represents an attempt to instill in the student the idea of continuing education and the need for constant attention to language throughout life.

3. Discussion

It can be seen from these extracts that we have kept the working of the unit and element headings largely free of vocabulary specific to a single occupation and we believe that by doing so we have a syllabus which, with variations in the profile, can be used for other technician courses including, automotive, civil, electrical and mechanical engineering technician courses. The descriptions of the various occupations will differ and so may the outline of the language setting and the targets but, for many technicians, their language needs will be covered by the units given above and the three subsequent units.

Sometimes, however, variations are needed in Unit One to meet the needs of certain occupations. A survey technician, for example, does not need
Element 01: Performing tests and experiments but will, instead, need an element
Element 01: Planning field and site surveys. He will, however, still need other elements including
Element 02: Estimating quantities and costs and
Element 04: Giving technical guidance. While he does not need Element 03 as he has no industrial plant to inspect he will need an equivalent element
Element 03: Regulating and adjusting survey instruments.

As we develop technician-level syllabuses we find more and more recurrent features in the main occupational events covered by the first unit of each syllabus: a mining survey technician will need the same language functions as an 'above-ground' survey technician. An instrumentation technician, who installs, maintains, regulates and repairs instruments in factories, has language functions which overlap those of the survey technician who regulates and adjusts survey instruments, and so on.

Language functions recur in surprising places and it is rare to find a unique requirement. A unit
Inspecting premises and examining food and food-preparation facilities which includes such elements as
Identifying oneself and outlining area of authority
and
Outlining steps to be followed during the inspection
and
Investigating complaints
is written as the first unit, representing the main event, for an environmental

health inspector but will, with variations, be suitable as a minor event for a magistrate, one of whose tasks is the inspecting of prisons.

As well as the recurrence of language functions in the first units of the Language of Work syllabuses for many technicians (other language functions recur as well as) it seems that all technicians need the language functions of Units Two to Five in their entirety: no matter what their occupation, all the technicians work in English with their colleagues, they all meet the general public, they all contribute to the smooth running of their organizations through meetings and the writing of memorandums and they all need to maintain and develop their technical standards. Thus four of the five units are common to all technicians and most elements of the first unit recur in many occupations. When there are variations, these, too, are rarely unique.

When we come to designing syllabuses for our second group of workers, the production and related workers, we find that many of the language functions given above are appropriate also for the productive trades. With minor exceptions
    Unit Two: Working with colleagues, supervisors and subordinates
    Unit Four: Contributing to the smooth running of the unit
and
    Unit Five: Maintaining and developing personal technical standards
all recur in the language needs of production workers.

The main differences between the technicians and the production workers are found in their actual work and in some aspects of their dealing with other people. The main occupational event of a machine operator, a fitter, a mechanic or a television repairman is the installation, maintenance and repair of equipment. With this event as a unit heading we can design a new first unit which includes the following activities:

    Ascertaining work to be done
        reading job sheet
        consulting foreman or supervisor
        consulting work manuals, plans or specifications
        diagnosing faults
    Estimating quantities and costs
        identifying materials and replacements needed
        identifying labour required
    Maintaining or repairing system or components
        requisitioning new components
        fixing and installing components
        testing completed work
        completing job sheet
    Controlling and guiding other workers
        outlining task to be accomplished

supervising work in progress
inspecting work in progress
testing completed work.

Each of these activities is then assigned appropriate language functions and a unit is built up which provides for the main occupational event of most production workers. Again, some of the elements above overlap with those of the technician.

Even when the main occupational event seems very different from the one given immediately above, the activities may still be appropriate for production workers like bricklayers, woodworkers or others. Their main event may be the installing of plumbing fixtures or the erection of wooden structures but the language functions remain the same as for those of the television repairman. A unit heading
    Installing or repairing plumbing fixtures
or
    Erecting and repairing foundations, walls and structures may be unique to a single occupation but the elements, the activities within the event, are a recurrence of those of a machine operator, a fitter or a mechanic. The plumber, like the machine operator, has to read a job sheet, consult with a foreman or supervisor, consult plans and specifications, diagnose faults, estimate costs, test finished items, complete a job sheet and supervise untrained workers. The wide variations in their actual work should not be allowed to disguise the continual recurrence of common language functions in the language of that work.

One difference between the technician and the production worker is that the production worker is often aiming at self-employment and will need the language notions for dealing directly with a customer. The lanuage must cover the following activities:

    Receiving the customer
        greetings
        identifying oneself
        establishing identity of customer
    Discussing customer's requirements
        identification of problem or need
        establishing agreement on work to be done
        giving quotations
    Completing the order
        re-contacting customer in case of need
        presenting account
        receiving payment.

When language functions are assigned to these activities, a language unit is built up which is common to all those who deal directly with a customer and which can usually replace the more general unit concerned with dealing with the general public. As it stands, a unit based on the activities listed immediately above can be used for a person operating a tailor's shop or a panel-beating yard. Additionally, with minor alterations, it can be used for people in the service industry and in clerical work like hotel receptionists or insurance clerks who come face-to-face with the customer.

Recognition of such recurrence, whether it is between the language functions of a health inspector and a magistrate or a hotel receptionist and a tailor, is helped if the unit and element headings are not masked by an elaborate use of technical terms specific to a single occupation.

It may seem that, through the use of recurrent features, the syllabuses are not specific enough and it must be admitted that they lack the detail of samples given by Munby (1978) or Hawkey (1980); but it must also be pointed out that these syllabuses are pre-experience syllabuses for the prototype technician or craftsman and do not take into account idiosyncratic elements of a single job in a single organization. It must also be stressed that these syllabuses take into account implementational constraints and represent what we hope can be covered under the most favourable circumstances that can be negotiated in terms of time, resources and in-service teacher training.

Conclusion

From the examples given above it can be seen that specificity does not necessarily imply uniqueness in ESP syllabus design. A large number of language events recur in a large number of different occupations and, even when an event seems specific to a single occupation, the activities within that event and the language functions required for those activities are common to more than one occupation. As one builds up a series of syllabuses, so one builds up a bank of activities and appropriate language skills and functions which allows for rapid and accurate ESP syllabus design.

Acknowledgements

I should like to acknowledge the work of my counterpart, Aaron Malama, who has been involved with me on all stages of our work in syllabus design but who was on study leave during the writing of this article. I should also like to acknowledge the support given by the British Council and the Department of Technical Education and Vocational Training, Zambia to our project in syllabus design and development in English for Specific Purposes (ESP) at technical and vocational level.

References

CANDLIN, C., KIRKWOOD, J. and MOORE, H. (1975) Developing study skills in English. In: *English for Academic Study*, ETIC Occasional Paper, British Council.

HAWKEY, R. (1980) Syllabus design for specific purposes. In: *Projects in Materials Design*, ELT Documents. The British Council.

INTERNATIONAL LABOUR OFFICE (1969) *International Standard Classification of Occupations.* ILO.

MUNBY, J. (1978) *Communicative Syllabus Design.* Cambridge University Press.

WILKINS, D. (1976) *Notional Syllabuses.* Oxford University Press.

WILLIAMS, R. (1973) A function-based course in English as a foreign language in science and technology. University of Lancaster, 1973 (mimeographed), quoted in Candlin, Kirkwood and Moore, 1975 (*op cit.*).

LANGUAGE IN LEGAL PRACTICE

H. WAINMAN and M. WILKINSON

University of Malawi

Introduction

We have been trying for the past two years to design a course directly related to the language needs of practising lawyers in Malawi. In this paper, we consider the background to legal training in Malawi, the initial decisions on course design, the attempts we have made to implement these decisions, and an evaluation of progress to date. Finally we consider some problems which remain very much with us.

1. Designing the Programme

The law course at this University has to fulfil two purposes. It has to offer a conventional legal academic education and, at the same time, provide a practical training so as to equip students with the necessary expertise to enter into legal practice directly upon graduation, the attainment of a law degree being the sole precondition to admission to practice. Further, unlike the legal profession in England, which is divided into solicitors and barristers fulfilling disparate functions, the profession in Malawi is fused. This means that the lawyer must be so trained that he combines the interviewing and drafting techniques of the solicitor with the pleading abilities of the barrister. The difficulties in respect of professional training in a country where the profession is fused have been encountered in many developing countries and clearly necessitate a wider curriculum than in countries with a bifurcated profession. Also in common with many developing countries is a teaching environment, where English is the official language of the courts and the medium of instruction in the secondary schools and University. Indeed English is almost a first language for many of our students.

The factors set out above largely dictated the nature and content of our course.

We should now put the legal English course in context within the law programme. The University system has opted for a common first-year programme, so the potential lawyer will not enter the law programme until his second year and he will continue law studies for a further four years before graduation and call to the Bar. During the common first year the student will receive English lectures in language and literature, the type of approach varying according to whether the philosophical whim of the moment looks to a liberal arts or a study skills approach. At the end of the first year, the students are examined in all subjects. Interested students may apply for admission to the law programme, entry being highly competitive and only those students with a high overall aggregate of marks are accepted. In view of the prominence that efficient use of English is accorded in the law programme, no student will be admitted without high grades in English.

The English for lawyers course is taught primarily throughout the first year of legal studies and it is this first-year course that forms the subject of this paper. There is a follow-up to the course in the final year, however, where some facets of the course — notably advocacy and drafting — are taught again in considerably more detail.

It seemed evident to us from the outset that student motivation had to be a key factor in course design. We take over second-year students, beginning a professional course, who believe that they have finished forever with English as a subject and who also believe they have sufficient language competence to flourish as lawyers. How then do we present a course which will recognize the language needs of the legal profession whilst at the same time maintaining interest for students who feel that the subject 'English' is now a little beneath them?

A possible solution was one we have seen adopted elsewhere. We could present academic texts of a legal nature and teach the students to recognize the language features of these texts in preparation for their final academic examinations. Such an approach would perhaps satisfy our academic law colleagues and the external examiner in law; the English teacher would feel on safer academic ground, despite our present limited knowledge of discourse analysis. We rejected such a method, however, because of its apparent sterility and decided that our approach must be 'purpose' not 'text' (Roe, 1981).

We agree with Roe: 'The most manageable unit of purpose for classroom management is the *task*' (p. 158).

How, then, do we clarify our 'task'? We could have conducted a detailed needs analysis (cf. Munby, 1978), but staffing ratios in the English Language Unit do not allow for such luxury and we are not that convinced of the efficacy of such an approach. We sat down, lawyer and English teacher, and talked out the main tasks lawyers would meet in a fused practice. Of course, not every lawyer will perform every task but, by introducing the tasks at this early stage in the course, the students can form an early opinion as to whether they are better suited to office work or court appearance, influencing their ultimate selection of a post in government, judiciary, or the private sector.

Close links are maintained between the Department of Law and the several facets of practice and, with widely sought advice, we decided on the following course components as representing the main language functions of a lawyer in Malawi: the legal interview, the legal letter, advocacy, comprehension and summary of judgments, and drafting of legal documents.

We found several lawyers justifying a course such as ours and emphasizing the need for language expertise in the profession, even in a mother-tongue situation. For example, Sir Henry Benson, addressing a trainee solicitors' conference in England in 1980, had this to say:

> You need to be proficient in your mother tongue. This is not merely a question of grammar; it is the skill in articulating clearly, without prolixity, in a logical sequence and in non-technical language, both orally and in writing.

Language expertise is of particular importance to a lawyer. We therefore spend some time in the opening to our local textbook, *Language in Legal Practice*, pointing out to our students the special nature of the language to which they are now being introduced.

We find it surprising that courses in the drafting of legal documents and advocacy do not find prominence in law curricula. The dearth of such courses has presumably arisen because of the difficulty of teaching such topics. There are too few rules immediately discernible. There are too few precedents for reference. Our teaching material has, therefore, to be largely original.

There was the added problem, occasioned by siting the course in the first year of legal studies, that the students knew little substantive law or procedure. The teaching had to involve real legal issues. It became apparent to us that the young lawyer handled these situations with greater confidence when the same problem was covered stage by stage. The same facts could be handled at the interview stage, follow-up letter, and presentation of the case in court. We also chose our legal situations with care to ensure that they were interesting, yet not too complex. If the student's understanding of the legal issues was shaky, his interview, letter, etc., clearly reflected this uncertainty and indeed amplified it. The final-year follow-up course will not be beset by this problem and more complex legal situations can be dealt with in confidence.

2. Implementation

The presentation of the course is now described in some detail. It should be remembered that we expected problems of motivation, and therefore we turn frequently to A.V. support as a deliberate contrast to the system of academic lectures in law.

(i) The legal interview

A lawyer's first meeting with his client is usually in the office. A lawyer must learn how to welcome his client, how to make him feel relaxed, often under conditions of stress, and then he must encourage the client to recount his story logically and accurately. Too many interruptions confuse, too few can lead to extreme prolixity and irrelevance. Most important, the lawyer must, where possible, know in advance what facts he is trying to ascertain, and therefore a check list is very useful once the interview begins. The experienced lawyer may carry the list in his head, but the inexperienced will need to have it written down and should refer to it frequently.

As teaching aids we prepared three interviews on sound tape. The first two are intended to illustrate badly conducted interviews, the first showing an ill-prepared lawyer who confuses his client and consequently fails to extract many of the pertinent facts, the second illustrating a totally unsympathetic lawyer whose manner would drive away many of his clients. Finally we prepared a suggested model interview.

The students are required to listen to the interviews in the language laboratory and criticize the interview techniques. They are also asked to prepare a list of questions that had been omitted. Finally they are required to deduce a check list that the lawyer would have used for the model interview.

In follow-up sessions we talk further about the techniques of interviewing, how to open up, how to control within a fixed time, how to gain thinking time, how to recapitulate, how to close on a positive note. We discuss the art of reassurance, persuasion, qualified agreement and advice.

Finally we put the students into groups and they act out interview situations, each taking on the role of lawyer and client, the client being thoroughly briefed in advance as to his story and the lawyer being warned in advance by letter of the nature of the subject matter of the interview to give him an opportunity to prepare the required check list. Other members of the group act as observers and critics.

(ii) The legal letter

The ability to write a clear and concise letter is important to a lawyer, being a permanent record of his competence and an advertisement of his abilities. An ill-drafted letter may have several unfortunate repercussions. The client may be confused as to his legal rights and may, in consequence, refrain from an action to enforce them. Alternatively he may feel, as a result of the letter, that he has a good case when, in fact, it is shaky. The letter must therefore give advice with precision, not an easy task. Further, an ill-drafted letter may cause a client to seek advice elsewhere and, if sent to a colleague in the profession, lower the reputation of the writer in the eyes of his colleagues.

Material was prepared on the assumption that our students would find it difficult to paraphrase and predict. We asked them to rephrase lawyers' letters that were badly written and to predict clients' letters when given the lawyers' replies. Finally, we asked students to draft letters in reply to clients' queries.

We could assume an all too familiar knowledge of business letter writing, but we thought it worth mentioning once again the principles of clarity with brevity, completeness and politeness, and the need to avoid 'officialese' or 'gobbledygook'. It is not easy for a lawyer to explain legal jargon in lay terms, even in a face-to-face situation, so it is all the more difficult when the recipient is at a distance.

As Sir Henry Benson said in the address referred to above,

> The main difference between an experienced practitioner and a novice is the singular inability of the novice to think like a client. He therefore puts points in oral discussion or in a letter without explaining the position clearly or considering what the client's reaction is likely to be. The result is that the client often does not understand. . . . If you put yourself in the client's shoes and ask yourself what his reaction will be, you will usually express yourself in a quite different and better way.

It is clearly inappropriate to use technical legal expressions in a letter to a lay client but often, as the students discovered, it is very difficult to avoid their use. How does one explain words like 'trust', 'settlement', 'executor' to a client? Through group work and frequent discussion we aim to counter examples such as the following:

Dear Mrs. Kamanga,

Thank you for the instructions as to the drafting of your will. I shall commence the task as soon as I have received the necessary clarification of a few points.

How old is your spouse? How many siblings do you have? Would you like me to arrange a settlement and if so who would you like to be the trustees? Do you want any remainders over if your spouse and siblings predecease you? Would you want the interests to vest only upon the happening of any contingencies, e.g. spouse not remarrying or children reaching 21?

Yours sincerely,
etc.

We speculated in our discussions, and we still speculate, on whether the legal profession, in a right desire to avoid ambiguity, is more prone than other professions to use unncessary jargon in its letters to clients.

(iii) Advocacy

Sound technique as an advocate is essential to the lawyer whose work involves court appearances. It has often been said that advocacy cannot be taught; such skill is innate. Not all lawyers agree.

Admittedly the truly great advocates — the Marshall Halls, the Norman Birketts and other forensic giants — were especially gifted from birth, but the vast preponderance of skilled and successful advocates have done little more than acquire a technique; and one, at that, which any person of reasonable intelligence and aptitude can acquire by patience, application and practice (Napley, 1975).

We turned to the language laboratory and closed-circuit television to help us in our task. For an opening exercise we encourage students to read selected judgments on to tape and then change booths and listen to each other. It is a chastening experience to hear one's own voice on tape and we remind students that this is the voice a judge will hear from the Bench. We try to help by pointing out how a spoken text can be divided into tone groups. We indicate the longer sense groups of descriptive prose as opposed to informal conversation and we point to the frequent falls in tone at the end of groups, indicative of the assertion of a judgment. We can also encourage the underlining of key words which will be given greater emphasis.

We follow on by presenting transcripts of court monologue (the submissions of counsel). By a careful perusal on the transcript, we can encourage students to recognize such features as extreme formality ('May it please your Lordship'), understatement ('I don't think I need to remind you'), polite insult ('I do not go so far as to make any comments about enlightened self-interest'), rhetorical questions ('one asks oneself where do the plaintiff's arguments end?'), etc.

It was appreciated that for our class of first-year students we could not conduct full mock trials, the students having no knowledge of procedure and evidence. We can, however, select various functions of a lawyer during a trial, such as examination-in-chief and cross-examination, and we can set up mock examinations of witnesses to give the students experience of these functions. The facts used in the examination of witnesses are the same facts already used for the interview and writing of letters so that the students approach with more confidence the legal issues involved. Once the student feels he can extract a simple story from a witness under the scrutiny of the court, we make the situation more difficult by instructing the witness to tell a different story from that told during the interview or to contradict himself, or to be deliberately confused. These tests are carried out in front of the television camera and we are able to play back and discuss the techniques used.

Examination-in-chief is followed by cross-examination of the witness by counsel instructed to represent the other party. Hence we are looking for an ability to use persuasion within the bounds of courtesy.

This is only intended to be a preliminary introduction to advocacy as the main instruction comes in the final year when we deal with the opening of the case, examination-in-chief, cross-examination, re-examination and submissions in detail. In this final year we have been very fortunate in having enormous support from the Bench, and mock and moot trials are conducted before members of the Judiciary. Clients are interviewed, proofs of evidence are taken from clients and witnesses, the pleadings are drafted and served, and interlocutory applications are heard before a member of the law staff posing as judge or master. A date is set for the hearing and the students then present their case as before a properly constituted court. The judge returns some days later to deliver his judgment. In this final year we are able to remind students that the language features we recognized in year one still apply.

(iv) Comprehension and summary of judgments

We turn to the written mode by asking students to read and summarize judgments delivered in the High Court of Malawi. It is an important test of a lawyer's skill that he should be able to peruse a judgment quickly and extract the *ratio decidendi* – the legal decision on the facts of the case. Students are encouraged through group work to work out a notation scheme for quickly marking off important sections. We can suggest, but not impose, a three-line marginal notation for the essential features, two lines for those of secondary importance, and a single line for points which are of interest, but do not strictly form part of the *ratio decidendi* – known technically as *obiter dicta*.

Naturally we encourage recognition of discourse features such as items in a list and exceptions to the argument, but such features are not always as apparent in local judgments as one might wish.

(v) Drafting

Our course comes to a conclusion with the drafting of legal documents, perhaps the most financially rewarding aspect of the lawyer's work, and certainly the most difficult.

Drafting is essentially a final-year course, but we feel that the language features of drafting should be introduced to the students at an early stage of their law course. By using 'cloze' technique on conveyancing documents, company agreements and legislative drafts, we can hope to discuss why certain words have to be used in certain contexts. We can then move on to layout features such as sub-headings and the numbering of clauses; we can consider stylistic features such as the long sentence structures, the numerous subordinate and often conditional clauses, the lack of punctuation where it would be expected, capitalization where it would not be expected, frequent repetition of important nouns, the reliance on the definite as opposed to the indefinite article, and the lack of adjectives and pronouns.

The final-year drafting course involves the students in drafting some of the more complex legal documents and, again, they are reminded of the language features mentioned in the first-year course.

The exercises that we have mentioned above are all aimed at improving language competence by allowing the students to roleplay the functions of the lawyer in practice. The techniques themselves cannot be taught thoroughly at this stage in the course and detailed instruction in several facets is left to the final practical year of teaching.

As we work in an environment which looks much, if not totally, to end-of-year examinations, with final scripts assessed by external examiners as an indication of student performance, we decided to examine, not in the conventional final three-hour examination, but by a series of tests extending throughout the final term.

We test the students' ability to interview by briefing outside clients on roles to be played. These clients are both Malawian and expatriate, because the lawyer will meet both in practice. The students do not know the full details of the case until they meet the client in the office, but they are told which part of the law the case will cover, or they are given a client's letter of enquiry outlining the legal issues in advance.

The students are told that we are looking for those features in the interview which we have discussed and practised earlier in the course. We both listen in to the interviews and they are also recorded on sound tape for assessment by the external examiner.

Similarly with advocacy, we present the students with outside witnesses for examination-in-chief and/or cross-examination and, again, we both assess, and the examinations are recorded, this time on video-tape. We also ask the students to make an unrehearsed recording of a judgment read on to tape in the language laboratory.

The written examination is more traditional. We expect the students to reply to letters from clients and redraft a badly written legal letter. We expect students to summarize judgments in the accepted legal manner and we expect them to summarize within a stated number of words. To date we have not tested drafting under examination conditions with first-year groups, but we do so in the final year.

For the past two years we have submitted all our work to the external examiner from the University of Oxford. He is a lawyer and we feel that, within such a specialized area, a lawyer is best suited to recognize the validity or otherwise of our work. Perhaps readers would care to comment on our decision.

3.   Evaluation

We find no precedents for a course such as ours and, as a result of our experiences, we have compiled a textbook for students, *Language in Legal*

Practice. This text is used continuously to supplement our lectures which are informally delivered, inviting as much discussion as possible. By dealing with work that the students will do in practice, the students recognize the relevance of the material and have not dismissed the course as peripheral. We have the added advantage of working with groups of no more than twelve students so that small group exercises are feasible. It would be very difficult to conduct the course if class numbers were much larger. We also see an advantage in sharing the teaching between a lecturer in language and a lawyer. Stress is thereby given to the language elements of the course and the law content can be properly apportioned.

Many problems remain. We feel we have not wholly convinced the traditional academic lawyer that our course is anything but lightweight. Universities deal traditionally in written assignments and not in video-tapes. Perhaps they always will. Our results do not always coincide with the results given out by the academic lawyers. Students do not find it easy to handle interviews and advocacy, and they feel more comfortable in the traditional written papers.

Nevertheless, if a lawyer is to be trained properly, it is essential that he is given instruction in such facets of his work as interviewing and argument in court. It is in these areas that appropriate use of language is so important and by no means can long study of law texts provide the confidence and poise required of the lawyer in practice. The lack of significant correlation between the marks of our language course and the substantive law marks has been noted. Perhaps, however, it merely reflects the fact that it is not necessarily the good academic lawyer who makes a good practitioner, but to evaluate with any certainty we will have to follow up the future careers of several of the students. Who does succeed in those professions where communication counts, the fluent performer or the one who knows his subject?

The art of the lawyer requires so much more than legal knowledge. Whether in an interview situation or whether pleading a case in court, legal knowledge alone will not win the day. Clear presentation, cogent argument and a pleasing manner are essential concomitants to legal knowledge if the lawyer is to succeed. We face the dilemma of all language teachers when we speculate on where language ends and subject knowledge begins.

References

BENSON, H. (1980) 'Professional efficiency'. Paper given at the Trainee Solicitors' Annual Conference, England.
MUNBY, J. (1978) *Communicative Syllabus Design*. Cambridge University Press, Cambridge.
NAPLEY, D. (1975) *The Technique of Persuasion*. Sweet and Maxwell, London, p. 1.
ROE, P. J. (1981) 'Fundamental Principles of E.S.P. Methodology', *Recherches et Échanges*, Tome 6, No. 2, pp. 1–10 and 158–159.

NOTES ON CONTRIBUTORS

Roger Bowers
Roger Bowers has been a British Council officer since 1964. After serving in Ghana and India and studying at Reading University (where he gained an MPhil and PhD) he was appointed in 1978 as Consultant in the Council's English Language Consultancies Department. In 1980 he took up the KELT post of Visiting Professor, Centre for Developing English Language Teaching, Ain Shams University, Cairo.

Peter Brown
Peter Brown read English at Liverpool and served as an Education Officer in the RAF before teaching in South Africa and Rhodesia. He was then Head of English at Prince of Wales School, Nairobi, and subsequently Headmaster of Allidina Visram School. He joined the British Council in 1971, and after taking his Dip.App.Ling. at Edinburgh, served as an ACE in Nigeria, as Deputy Representative in Argentina, and in English Language Consultancies in London. He resigned from the Council in 1978 and returned to Kenya in 1979 as KELT Officer at the University of Nairobi.

David Clarke
David Clarke obtained his BA in 1972 and PGCE in 1973 at London University. He was awarded an MA in EFL/ESL from the University of Wales. Bangor, in 1979. He went on to teach ESP at IAP, Oran, Algeria, English at Bugandi High School, Plae, Papua New Guinea, and ESP at the University of Khartoum, Sudan. He was involved in the implementation of the KELT Textbook Project in Mogadishu, Somalia, where he is at present working.

James Drury
James Drury spent two years teaching in England after graduating from the University of London. He then gained EFL and ESL experience teaching in Libya and Swaziland for five years. He returned to SOAS, University of London, for an MA in Linguistics and then worked as Senior Lecturer in the English Language Unit of Ngoe Ann Technical College, Singapore. He is currently a KELT Officer in the Department of Educational Communications and Technology, Kenyatta University College, Nairobi: involved specifically in language course design and implementation for teacher-trainees.

Neville Grant
Neville Grant taught at Dar es Salaam Technical College and Dar es Salaam

Teachers' College between 1964 and 1968 before joining the British Council as an English Language Officer. He lectured at the University of Lagos College of Education until 1973. Since that time he has worked as a full-time educational writer and consultant. He is the author of many books and has done work for the BBC and the Open University, as well as a variety of assignments for the British Council in such places as Morocco, Sierra Leone, Czechoslovakia and Brazil.

Anne Hayes

Anne Hayes has been a British Council Officer since 1970. She taught at the Council's English Language Teaching Institute in London, and in Turkey. She has undertaken teacher-training assignments in Peru, Denmark, Greece, France and Italy, and in 1980 she took up an advisory KELT post in Sierra Leone. She will work until 1984 on the project described in her article.

Ian Harrison

Ian Harrison read Modern Language at Oxford before studying for a PGCE (TESL) at Bangor. After spending two and a half years teaching French in Britain he went to Zaire to lecture in English Language, Linguistics and Methodology. He then worked for the national airline in Saudi Arabia, training pilots, mechanics and communicators before going to the University of Leeds to obtain an MA in ELT and Linguistics. He is at present a provincial English Inspector in Cameroon where he has been since 1978. He is co-author of the three-year course for Cameroonian Francophone primary schools (Living Together).

Harry Hawkes

Harry Hawkes was awarded an MA from St. Andrews Univesity in 1965, and an MA in TEFL/Linguistics from Leeds University in 1971. He taught in intermediate and secondary schools in Libya between 1965–68, was ELT Regional Inspector in Libya (1968–70), Head of English at Bagabaga Secondary Teacher Training College, Tamale, Ghana (1971–75). At Universidad Nacional de Trujillo, Peru, from 1975 to 1980 he was visiting lecturer (British Technical Assistance) and was Teacher Training Advisor of the KELT Textbook Project, Mogadishu, Somalia.

Stuart Hirst

Stuart Hirst took up land agency after leaving Oxford. He first taught EFL in Brighton, later in summer schools for UNESCO in Poland, and privately in Turkey. He took his MA in Applied Linguistics at Essex in 1970. He taught at the University of Libya (Benghazi) and then at Haile Selassie University, Addis Ababa, where his stay was cut short by the revolution. He had further lessons in survival on the British Council PES project at King Faisal University, Damman, Saudi Arabia. He has been a KELT officer in the Language and Study Skills Unit at the University of Nairobi since 1978.

Leo O'Keeffe
Leo O'Keeffe has worked in London as a teacher in a comprehensive school, in Fiji as an Education Officer, in Ethiopia as a Research Fellow at the University, in Kuwait as English Language Officer with the British Council and he is now working in Zambia under the KELT scheme. He has an MA in Applied Linguistics from Essex University and an MA in Curriculum Development and Educational Technology from Sussex University.

Norman A. Pritchard
Norman Pritchard has a BA (1961) and Dip.Ed. (1962) from Leicester University and an MA in Applied Linguistics (1973) from Essex University. His teaching positions include: teacher of English in Oxted County School; Assistant d'Anglais at CEG Augruico, France; Head of English at Manama Technical School, Bahrain; Head of English at Sekolah Alam Shah, Kuala Lumpur. He was a visiting specialist to King Faisal Univesity, Saudi Arabia, and British Council Centre, Isfaham, Iran. As well as his involvement in the KELT Project, Magadishu, Somalia, he is a textbook writer, and was an adviser in ESP at Kabul University, Afghanistan.

Jacky Pritchard
Jacky Pritchard studied at Coventry Art College. She has taught EFL and General English in Bahrain, Malaysia and Somalia. From 1976 to 1979 she worked as illustrator to the KELT Textbook Project in Afghanistan and is now illustrator to the KELT Project, Somalia. In her spare time she free-lances as a Graphics Consultant for UN projects.

Pauline Rea
Pauline Rea has taught English and trained teachers in Francophone Africa — Burundi (1960–70) and Zaire (1971–73). She worked at the Colchester English Study Centre (1973–74) before studying Applied Linguistics at the University of Lancaster (1974–75). She then worked at Lancaster as a research associate on the General Medical Council Language Testing Project (1975–76) and as lecturer in the Institute for English Language Education responsible for curriculum development, syllabus design and language testing (1976–78). Since the end of 1978 she has worked as Co-ordinator of the Communication Skills Unit and Senior Lecturer in the Department of Foreign Languages and Linguistics at the University of Dar es Salaam.

Brian Smith
Brian Smith obtained his MA in Cambridge, PGCE in London and Dip TESL in Leeds. From 1953 to 1963 he was Educational Officer in Malaysia. Since joining the British Council in 1963 he has served in ELT posts in Bangladesh, Nigeria, Indonesia and Venezuela. He is currently project leader of the Textbook Project and ELT Adviser in Somalia.

Harry Wainman
Harry Wainman has been teaching English in Africa and the Middle East for twenty years. He is at present a KELT Officer and Head of the English Language Unit at Chancellor College, University of Malawi.

Roy Wigzell
Roy Wigzell began his career over twenty years ago as a teacher of English in Somalia. He has a PhD in General Linguistics from the University of Manchester and has taught both Applied Linguistics and Theoretical Linguistics at a number of universities in Britain and Africa. Since 1973 he has been an Associate Professor of English at the University of Oslo. At the time the present article was written, he was on secondment under the British Council KELT scheme to the University of Zambia.

Michael Wilkinson
Michael Wilkinson, an English barrister, was the head of the first postgraduate professional law-training course in Uganda, and is presently Head of the Law Department in the University of Malawi.

Paul Wilson
After reading English at Oxford, Paul Wilson taught in London for three years before going to Northern Nigeria to work in a Teacher Training College. From there he went to Cairo as a lecturer in the Institute of the Education, Ain Shams University. He returned to England for a year to teach in a secondary modern school, and then went to Morocco where he became and adviser in teacher training. After Morocco he returned to England a second time, taught for four years at a comprehensive school, obtained an MA in ELT and Linguistics at Leeds and went out to Cameroon in 1978 as a Teacher Training Expert. He is co-author of *Living Together*, the three-year course for Cameroonian francophone primary schools.